THE NATURALIST IN LAKELAND

THE NATURALIST IN
Lakeland

ERIC HARDY

DAVID & CHARLES: NEWTON ABBOT

0 7153 5745 X

Set in 12 on 13 point Bembo
and printed in Great Britain
by Latimer Trend & Company Ltd
for David & Charles (Holdings) Limited
South Devon House Newton Abbot Devon

Contents

List of Illustrations

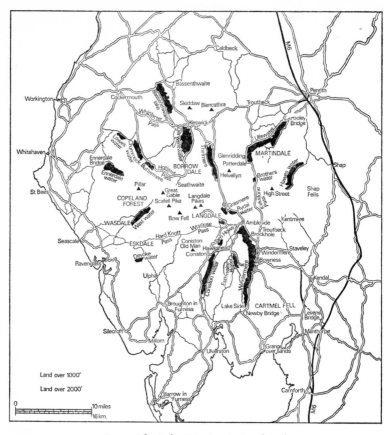

Fig 1   The Lake District National Park

CHAPTER ONE

Introduction

ENGLAND'S TALLEST MOUNTAINS and largest lakes lie across Cumbria, the former Cumberland, Westmorland and north Lancashire, an area of silence and solitude, where much of the wildlife lives as it did in prehistoric times. Lancashire's previous share of Lakeland included Coniston and Esthwaite Waters, three-quarters of the shores of Windermere, the southern side of Langdale Tarn, the larchwoods at Skelwith Bridge where cross-bills breed at times, and England's finest deer forest, at Grizedale.

Lakeland's National Park (created in 1951) does not contain all the best flora and fauna, and proposals have been made to extend it. Energetic birdwatchers may winter with Solway's hordes of wildfowl and climb for golden plover, and perhaps dotterel, at the source of Tyne and Tees along the region's Pennine border. The limestone flora is richest where Teesdale violet and western spiked speedwell maintain outposts at Arnside and Humphrey Head, on the southern border, and Britain's largest breeding colony of nine pairs of bitterns flourishes at nearby Leighton Hall Moss, birds and flowers forming part of the ecology of north Morecambe Bay. Morecambe Bay is a major haunt of migratory waders and south Solway of grey geese, and bird-counts show that a large proportion of Britain's sanderling and ringed plovers make the peak of their migration in May, via the estuaries from Morecambe Bay and Esk to Solway.

Naturalists may see four species of deer roaming wild among

Lakeland's thirty-seven land mammals. England's only Scottish-style deer-stalking forest, up Martindale, however, allows less natural observation of wild deer than do the tree-top hides in the silent, windless conifer country of Grizedale or Scaife Heights, the red deer's natural habitat. The pine-marten ranges above tree level, though it benefits from afforestation and conservation, and the reduction of trapping. Its diet consists mainly of field voles, augmented by small birds, beetles and autumn berries, now that squirrels are scarcer; it is interesting as a host for round worms or flat worms, and as an example of the evolution of delayed implantation, which allows it to breed during the early summer. After mating in July or August, implantation of the blastocyst takes place in spring, seven or eight months later, and parturition twenty-seven days afterwards. Such an animal is worth conserving, and it may yet be needed to check grey squirrels and American mink invading from the south.

The golden eagle is now one of the 300 or so wild birds. Since World War II black-tailed godwits have bred along the Solway, harriers on the afforested border Pennines, golden oriole and siskin in the forest and bitterns in the southern reed-beds, while merganser and goosander have spread from Scotland inland along the rivers and lakes. The high crags remain the stronghold of England's peregrines, ravenages increase annually, blackcock and buzzard thrive upon afforestation. The erection of nest-boxes has allowed redstarts and pied flycatchers to spread through wood and dale that offer few natural nest-holes for them. Greylag and Canada geese have been introduced to many waters where sandpipers are a feature of summer. Noisy sea-birds crowding St Bees cliffs in summer now have black guillemots and fulmars, while Europe's biggest ground colony of herring and lesser black-backed gulls nests on Walney Island. Drigg Point, commonly misnamed Ravenglass, harbours one of Britain's largest colonies of black-headed gulls and Sandwich terns. Hordes of autumn oystercatchers, the greatest wader flocks in Britain, feed on the cockle beds and other shellfish in Morecambe Bay, while vociferous pinkfooted geese from Iceland invade the Solway sky, the greatest goose-haunt in the country. Greylags flock in the Kent estuary.

Grass snakes and adders still live in Grizedale and adders have also been found near Penrith, Lever's Water, High Nibthwaite and Witherslack. A grass snake 2ft 6in long was found at Frith, near Grizedale, in 1964, and others at Roudsea Wood. Atlantic salmon home to six Lakeland rivers. The Ice Ages that shaped the region left arctic flowers and sedges, the mountain-ringlet butterfly on the hilltops, and migratory arctic char and Coregonid whitefish landlocked in its cold deep lakes, where they have evolved local subspecies. Northern herring and southern bass migrate into the Cumbrian Sea, part of a food-chain of marine life upon which bird-watchers as well as seabirds and shorebirds depend in a balance of populations easily upset by chemical as well as oil pollution drifting from Liverpool Bay's shipping channels, the industries at Barrow and the chemical effluents tipped from half England's industry into the Irish Sea.

Lakeland's 1,382 *Lepidoptera* have of course many more moths than butterflies. From Windermere to Witherslack fly satin carpet moths. Spotted yellow balsam (*noli tangere*) flowering in damp woods by Windermere, Coniston, Derwentwater and Buttermere, and by Rusland, Rydal, Keswick and Ambleside roadsides, is the sole food of Britain's last netted carpets, now that these moths are extinct in North Wales. Cliburn Moss in the Eden valley is a southerly haunt of the grey mountain carpet moth, while you may find Haworth's carpet at Grange-over-Sands and the bedstraw carpet at Witherslack. Great brocades migrate from Scandinavia over the Pennines to Penrith. Beautiful snout and red-necked footman occur at Roudsea Wood, the latter ranging to Newby Bridge. Eskdale has large nutmeg moths, and Grange has marbled coronets. Glaucous shears at Holker, the double dart at Roudsea and the scarce dagger at Witherslack—such names are a tribute to the interest these moths once attracted. Cartmel and Newby Bridge have satin lutestrings, Grange has white satins, while there are shark moths and large wainscots at Holker Moss.

Connoisseurs of the area's large insects may find 1,894 beetles, food for bats, buzzards and others. There are 20 different dragonflies, and trout-anglers can count 24 species of mayfly dancing over their rivers. From the Duddon Valley to Ashness Wood at Keswick, the northern wood-ant *lugubris* may be noticed by its nests of pine needles, and at Silverdale and Arnside the southern wood-ant *rufa* builds its hillocks. In recent years the sawfly *Phymatocera aterrima* has spread to Grasmere.

Rare caddis-flies like *Limnephilus xanthodes* inhabit Blelham Bog, and the white-beaked sedge protects the large heath butterfly's caterpillar at Meathop Moss. The elimination of orchard pests like appleblossom weevil by the use of insecticides has not overcome lamentations at the loss of the wood white butterfly (near Carlisle), the chalk hill blue (at Grange) and the brown hairstreak.

A lavish growth of parsley fern flourishes on rocky ridges and in gullies facing west. American monkey-musk and New Zealand willowherb line the banks of streams. Lichens encrust the precipices and rock slabs, testimony to the absence of industrial pollution. Cloudless skies in early June urge the alpine botanist to emulate the mountain goats of Coniston and Tilberthwaite and reach basic rocks, where England's finest alpine flowers grow. For less energetic plant hunters, the region's southern limestone has an equally rich flora, enlivened by the flight of argus and fritillary, brimstone and hairstreak butterflies.

The weather has profound effects on wildlife: as an instance, in the abnormally cold wet June of 1972 two peregrine eyries were lost, as were many young lapwings, grouse and other ground nestlings. Yet possession of England's highest rainfall, a major influence upon the distribution of plants and insects, has earned Lakeland an unnecessarily bleak reputation among would-be visitors. Despite the unenviable figure of 131in per annum at Seathwaite Tarn, north of the Wastwater–Borrowdale Pass, rainstorms are often very localised, autumn to new year being usually the wettest period. The central mountains of folded and faulted Older Palaeozoic rocks receive most rain, with an average of 150in at 2,800–3,000ft. From here the isobars radiate roughly in concentric circles outwards. Most rain is brought on south-westerly winds; but rainfall depends much upon elevation. Seathwaite had 3in one September day in 1971 and Styhead averages 170in, whereas Keswick averages 58in and Carlisle 32in. Lakeland's rainfall grows conifers and deciduous trees that are taller and more luxuriant than the same species in drier East Anglia.

The mildest winter climate borders Morecambe Bay. (In the severe frost in February 1963 I found little ice on the roads until Newby Bridge.) February is the coldest month, especially on the eastern border and at Carlisle, where the northeasterly helm-wind is notorious. The whole of Lake Windermere froze in February 1895, but not again until the great frost of February 1929, when it safely supported 50,000 skaters. The ice dispersed its waterfowl to Morecambe Bay. Spring floral isophenes, or lines of equal flowering dates, are earliest from Morecambe Bay along west Cumberland to Solway, as early as western Lanca-shire and North Wales. Then they graduate inland with iso-phenes running south to north. Spring bird-migrant isophenes, or lines of equal arrival dates, are different. The earliest border Morecambe Bay, equalling the Lancashire coast and north Anglesey. They next include the Cumberland coastal area, and move inland to the Pennines. Leighton Moss receives some of Britain's earliest garganey by mid-March, when ring-ouzels reach the western fells.

Too few naturalists know Lakeland in winter, when railway excursions run half empty and there is room to walk on the pavement at Ambleside. Wild geese roam the Solway sky, and wild swans visit the tarns until they freeze, then move on to the deeper lakes. Great grey shrikes return to favoured territories, and sometimes a blackcap left over from the summer visits one of the many garden bird-feeders, or a sandpiper favours the waters of the southern Crake. The harsh grating song of the dipper can be heard along the Eden rushing through its lovely gorge at Wetheral, until the river in spate forces the bird up the quieter becks. Tufted duck and goldeneye now replace the noisy speedboats on the lakes, and deers' footprints can be seen in the snow. Mountain hares turn creamy white along the Northumbrian border, herring enter the Solway, while barnacle geese flock to the Duddon and greylags to Meathop.

In the restless weather of spring, when trout have lost their long lean look of winter and fresh-run salmon vault their way up the Eden, Daphne laurel flowers as far north as Ivy Crag Wood, Under Skiddaw. In June squinancy wort flowers in its northernmost European haunt in Westmorland. Snow may lie 2in deep when ring-ouzels return with March, and curlews and oystercatchers move inland from Morecame Bay. At Rydal, Dora's Field bursts into a golden host of hybrid daffodils, which conservationists try to preserve from avaricious collectors. There are primroses, bluebells and anemones in the woods. Then, sometime in April, curlews and golden plovers are heard over the fells, and, below Cartmel, brimstone butterflies awake from their hibernation.

Spring slips into summer with the short flowering season of alpine flowers. The mayfly hatches here in June, but the anglers are preceded by bands of campers and hikers. Climbers start pulling plants from their footholds, and disturbing the peregrines on Ennerdale Crag, or nesting buzzards. Fortunately, birds of prey usually keep alternative nesting sites, where they may re-lay their eggs with better success. Summer is the most testing time for wildlife. Yet many birds and animals are increasing in number. Afforestation, despite its critics, has encouraged roe deer and blackcock, and proved the salvation of red squirrels; and green woodpeckers have extended into the south around Yewdale and goosanders into the north. It seems that the modern conservationist can still preserve a healthy environment for wildlife, despite the invasion of Man.

In autumn the bracken on Shap Fell turns russet and the Furness forests red. Martindale stags return to roar on Rampside, the summer haunt of hinds, and the odd stag driven from the rut in Grizedale may wander across Crinkle Crags at the

Page 17 (*above*) Elterwater, a haunt of wild swans and mergansers; (*below*) St Bees South Head, a summer seabird colony

Page 18 (*left*) A young badger shown at night at the entrance to its artificial sett, rehabilitated by Mrs Jane Ratcliffe after persecution in the Midlands; (*below*) a Forestry Commission badger-gate in a dry-stone wall in use at night

head of Langdale. Curlews leave the moorland to the grouse-shooters and fly to the coast. The first wild geese come noisily over Dunmail Raise on their way between Solway and the Kent estuary, sometimes dropping down by Bassenthwaite below Crosthwaite Church. The fells are silent now that lambing is over and the curlews have departed. Cock salmon show some of the same red as the trees as they approach their spawning beds. Ornithologists organise duck-counts on the lakes and wader-counts in the estuaries. Freshwater biologists may be studying ancient deposits of plankton on the bed of Windermere to find out how much the sewage-salts drained into the lake from human dwellings in the eighteenth and nineteenth centuries increased certain diatoms there.

To understand the lakes and fells, forests and dales, it is not enough to catalogue their flora and fauna. One's pleasure lies in coming to know why plants grow where they do and in observing mammals wild and free. There is splendid scope in the various districts to see how rocks and soils, exposure to westerly rain, elevation or shelter, influence the types of vegetation and animal life. To avoid repetition, Lakeland is in subsequent chapters considered in its major wildlife habitats.

Under the local government boundary reorganisation, the Lakeland area of Cumberland, Westmorland and north Lancashire 'north of the Sands', and Yorkshire's Howgill Fells, a corridor link of the Whinfell Hills, Birkbeck Fell, Bretherdale and Roundthwaite Common, Ravenstonedale and Mallerstang Common, become Cumbria. This does not include the Scottish portion of the ancient British Cumbria, which extended to Strathclyde in Arthurian times, so only part of the Solway Firth is in the new region.

B

CHAPTER TWO

Geology

Rocks

THE CONFUSION OF rocks that confronts climber, walker or motorist in Lakeland was created 500 million years ago in Ordovician times, when there were violent earthquakes and intense volcanic activity. Much later came a million years of grinding out the present scenery by glaciers which, up to 14–25,000 years ago, flowed down from Hellvellyn's Striding Edge, ground out the jaws of Borrowdale, smoothed out the rock at Grange and Grasmere's Red Bank and made rivers, until finally moving down the Solway coast. Glaciers came south from Scotland across Solway to carve lakes and dales, leaving ridges of glacial sand and gravel that turned several rivers parallel with the coast and denied the motorist a continuous coast road.

More recently came attacks by frost and rain, and now the boots of many walkers are wearing out the mountains. Northern-central Lakeland is mainly Skiddaw slates, then Borrowdale volcanics north of Windermere, in one central sheet to Keswick, not broken up like the volcanic rocks of Wales. South of Ambleside the skyline is Upper Silurian rock resting on the earlier slates and volcanics, with the soft fells of Coniston, Kendal and Windermere, and south of it Cartmel limestone. The fells do not come down to the southern coast because the rock beneath Morecambe Bay and Walney (except for limestone under the mouth of the Duddon) is sandstone and not the slate of the central hills; we see this New Red Sandstone in Holker Hall and the stumps of Furness Abbey, it rises up at St Bees Head and is in the Eden Valley and the Carlisle Plain, claimed to be formed nearly 200 million years ago. Penrith sandstone, of Permian Age, has evenly rounded grains betraying its desert origin. Sandstone was used for building the cathedral at Carlisle and its castle's red walls. Carboniferous limestone marks the Upper Eden Valley. Lakeland is largely a central volcanic mass fringed by limestone on the north-east and south, and by sandstone on the west, south-west and north-east. These steep, craggy central mountains of hard, volcanic rock therefore appear surrounded by rounder, softer hills, a contrast of bleak hills and fertile pastures. Erratic boulders wandering in the glacial drift travelled far from Lakeland. A ton of Cumberland volcanic andestic agglomerate came to rest outside Wavertree Library, Liverpool; 100 boulders found in a claypit at Great Crosby on the south Lancashire coast included Coniston Grit or other Silurian rocks from Lakeland, Borrowdale felspathic ash and felstone, pink syenite from Ennerdale and Lakeland basalt and dolerite. Others from the Lancashire Bootle included pink Eskdale granite.

Glaciers also carried boulders from Lakeland through the Stainmore and Tyne gaps 150 miles into Yorkshire (the way the shelduck route their summer moult-migration to the North Sea); down Lunesdale into Lancashire and along the coast to the Isle of Man, to Wales, the Mersey, the Midlands and to Norfolk. They made the combes and scratched out flat-bottomed valleys, removing rock and debris and leaving in west Lancashire Britain's broadest plain of drift-covered Triassic, extending to the sea. Borrowdale volcanics reached Hartlepool and Cambridge; Shap granite travelled down Teesdale; Cumberland's grey felspar and porphyry reached Aylesbury; and Eskdale granite boulders were found at West Park in Macclesfield, 120 miles away in Cheshire, down the Severn Valley at Worcester, and at Oxford. Buttermere granophyre was found in the form of small boulders when brickworks were dug for clay on the edge of Liverpool. Once bold features of Lakeland were softened by glaciers grinding down the Duddon Valley and Eskdale. Unusually heavy rainfall in 1966 brought many boulders down into Great Langdale and Borrowdale.

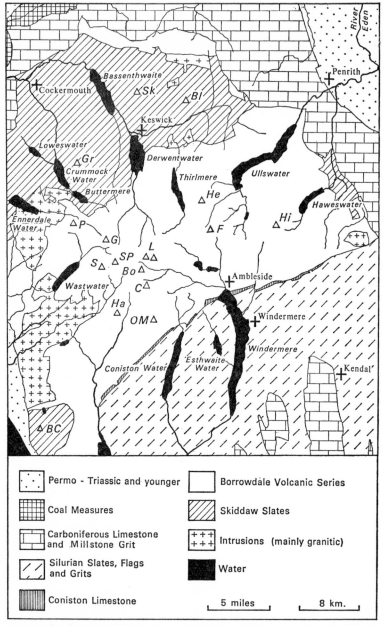

Fig 2 Sketch map of the geology of the Lake District (*based on ¼in sheet 3 and sheets 5 and 6 of the Geological Survey of Great Britain, by permission of the Director, Institute of Geological Sciences*)

The Drunken Duck on the Tarn Hows road was a favourite
Easter gathering place for geologists, who saw in the rocks more
than building material and Shap paving stone to be exploited in
quarry-gashed hillsides as at Coniston, and deplored the extraction of water-worn limestone from Hampsfell, near Grange-
over-Sands, and from Holme Park Fell. Lakeland grows its
alpine plants largely on volcanic ash. Its hard mountain edges
make it England's major breeding haunt of peregrine, ring
ouzel and raven, and supply the country's only eagle eyrie.
Frost and gales, rain and spray, have furrowed St Bees' New Red
Sandstone head, providing the only nesting-ledges in the region
for auks, kittiwakes, shags and fulmars. The iron-free limestone
pavements of the south nourish the richest flora and *Lepidoptera*,
and the glacial lakes the landlocked char and vendace, survivors
of pre-glacial fish-runs.

The soils, formed of course by rock erosion, have been
reddened by iron, blackened by peat, stiffened by glacial drift,
the boulder clay of Pleistocene times, or lightened by sand and
glacial or post-glacial alluvium to make the fertile meadows—
enriched by the humus of dead vegetation. The consequent
variety of flora explains why the naturalist's interest in landscape
goes beyond the lakes and mountains.

This north-western corner of England is packed with the
finest and most varied scenery, from the complex of Skiddaw's
towering mass of tilted slate to volcanic Borrowdale—a landscape modified first by ice, which formed Morecambe Bay, then
by water and finally by Man's exploitation of stone and minerals.
Stand on Keswick's Castle Rigg and you will see a number of
old volcanoes, the scenic feature about Derwentwater. Volcanic
rock has made the cliffs behind Grange-in-Borrowdale, quarried
near Cockermouth's Watch Hill. Slate has been quarried in
Borrowdale. Geological monuments range from stones in
Hadrian's Wall, where the Romans pushed their conquest
beyond Carlisle, to the Bowder Stone, a perched block in
Borrowdale; to the Basalt Crag of columnar basalt in the
Borrowdale series a few hundred yards south-west of Rainor's

Farm, near Gosforth; to Ennerdale's Pillar, with its alpine plant-relics; and to lesser rocks with bields (holes) for foxes or anchorage for slow-growing silvery lichen.

Windermere, England's largest lake, nestles among the Silurian slates, flagstones and gritstones of southern Lakeland, and is shallow only around Belle Isle. Some 20,000 years ago a great glacier, combining with smaller glaciers from Langdale, Rydal, Scandale and Stock Gyhll, pushed its way into the northern end of a former river valley here and deepened it still more. The river came from the mountains to the north, like the glaciers, but instead of following the present course of the River Leven, which drains Windermere to the sea at Greenodd, it reached the sea a little west of Grange-over-Sands. The terminal moraine at Newby Bridge, which twists the Leven's neck soon after it leaves the lake, marks the spot where the glacier turned to the south-east corner of the valley at Fell Foot, to grind its way into Morecambe Bay over the flatter land (which it made flatter still) past Staveley, leaving an excellent location for marsh plants between Hell Foot and Hazelrigg. North of Bowness, a branch off the main glacier gouged out the Winster Valley into the Kent estuary; the shallow bed at Belle Isle shows where its powers weakened. South of Belle Isle it received another tributary, the Esthwaite glacier, which strengthened it again.

The site of Windermere was a shallow sea 350 million years ago. The glacier gave Lake Windermere an average depth of 78ft and a maximum of 219ft off Wray Castle. The lake goes 91ft below sea-level, but its 12,250cu ft of water was not sufficient for thirsty cities and its surface level had to be raised; conservationists suggested that this scheme could replace the Morecambe Bay barrage, but it is doubtful whether enough water could be stored.

The hard Borrowdale volcanics, weathering bleak and craggy, are 350 to 380 million years old. The Skiddaw slates came from the mud and grit of an inland Palaeolithic sea about 450 million years ago, hardened by intrusions and earth movements over Ordovician rock. 'Brathay Black', the world's hardest commercial slate is quarried near Ambleside. Part of Lancashire's Black Combe, a whaleback of slates, volcanic rocks and granite dominating the Duddon Valley, has probably the oldest rock, reputed by some geologists to be pre-Cambrian, or at least very early Cambrian, as may be some of Skiddaw (because of its fossils), up to 600 million years old. Sandstone at St Bees and Penrith, and the small streamside Liassic outcrop near Carlisle, are claimed to be not more than 70 million years old, though other estimates are nearer 200 million.

Looking north round the head of Windermere, one notices the prominent Borrowdale volcanics, the bedded ash of old volcanoes belonging to the Ordovician series of up to 500 million years ago; they run from the south of Derwentwater, including Sty Head and Wasdale, and from the foot of Ullswater to Egremont. These compact rocks of central Lakeland form steep ragged weather-resisting crags like Helvellyn, Wansfell, Loughrigg, Bowfell, Great Dodd, Great Gable and Langdale's Pikes, quite unlike the lower, gentle and softer Silurian hills of Windermere and Ambleside. The centre's older granites and volcanic greenstones lack limestone, which affects the plant life as well as the scenery. Soft black mud-shales underlie the smoothly weathered slopes of Skiddaw, Blencathra and Whinlatter Pass, though central Lakeland consists mostly of the Borrowdale series of hard volcanic ash, extending to the south end of Derwentwater, flanked on both sides by the softer Silurian. The eastern part of Scafell, England's highest mountain, which towers over Hard Knott Pass above Eskdale, is granite, the western part Borrowdale volcanic. Volcanic ash, the remains of craters long gone, appears on the slopes of Striding Edge. These grim laval slabs and gullies of Borrowdale volcanics, the craggy sides of Great Gable (an unusually large unit of crag and scree), and the central fells were formed after the Skiddaw slate, which is mostly Ordovician. Thirlmere valley consists of rocks of the Borrowdale volcanic series, a thick pile of lava sheets and hard ash.

The boundary between the more complex Skiddaw group

and the Borrowdale volcanic group is best explained as a major
unconformity, according to a recent study by Helm and Roberts,
who suggest that the former group underwent extensive de-
formation before the deposition of the latter. There is still
controversy over the evidence from Crookley Beck, the north-
west margin of the Black Combe inlier, and the Grange-in-
Borrowdale exposures on the south margin of the Skiddaw
group at Scarbrow Wood and above Hollows Farm.

The Ordovician slates of the north stretch from east to west
as far as Keswick in roundish hills, except for the long razor-like
ridge of Saddleback (Blencathra), one of the easiest walker's
climbs, where the cleavage plane and bedding plane coincide
with the angle or the slope of the hill. Under the heathery
Carrock Fell, the Skiddaw slate meets the volcanic series in a
rich variety of fox-haunts in rocks and boulder-scree. Undulat-
ing granite intrudes into the Shap and Eskdale areas, probably
from the more recent Devonian age, with boulder-clay and
alluvial deposits of Pleistocene times. There is a strip of such a
composition near the summit of Scafell and patches in Skiddaw
Forest, behind Saddleback, and there are granite quarries at
Threlkeld.

The Ambleside–Coniston road marks the boundary between
the hard Ordovician and the softer upper Silurian of up to 440
million years ago, including the slates of Kendal, Coniston and
south Windermere. The hard rock of Ordovician High Yewdale, Coniston Old Man and Wetherlam stands above this
Silurian landscape, whose broad outcrop includes the Bannerdale beds of the fells above Cartmel to Newby Bridge, and
those beyond Lindale and Eller How.

Coniston slate in the Silurian can be light, dark or blue-grey.
In addition to the famous Coniston green roofing slate, there is
green Honister slate, and Broughton and Elterwater have green-
slate quarries. Coniston's 300ft deep Broughton Moor green-slate
quarries, 1,300ft above the road from Torver to Broughton-
in-Furness, present the landscape with a problem of waste.
Coniston limestone, on which grows the pink-eyed *Primula*

farinosa, is a narrow strip of compacted marine shells slanting east-north-east to west-south-west.

The Carboniferous period, some 350,000 years ago, left us the lovely flower-rich limestone hills of the south from Cartmel to Silverdale, and those of the Upper Eden, like Orton and Great Asby Scars and Aisgill. Pressed up from the old seabed near Grange-over-Sands, Lower Carboniferous limestone—pink, grey or bone-white—built the spur of Humphrey Head with its relict flora; Kirk Head with its horseshoe vetch, moonwort and flea-sedge; Cartmel, Yewbarrow, Meathop and Cat Crag fells; Whitbarrow, Yewdale, Underbarrow and Scout Scars; and the 800ft stone plateau of Hampsfell. They were shaped first by waves at their base, then by ice and rain on their tops. They are often full of shell fragments and broken corals used to divide otherwise very similar limestone, like the arching cliff on Arnside shore below Westholme, the oldest local limestone, and that along the shore to Gibraltar Point.

There is a geological fault along the central valley of this southern border from Sandside through Silverdale Station to the coast, where the rock is often turned up to stand on end, inclining to the north-east on the west side of the steep hills like Arnside Knott, but with gentler slopes to their east. Large crags like Warton on the east of this fault are steep to the south but slope gently to the north. Fine deciduous woods flourish in the glacial clay of the valleys below. Widespread submergence during Neolithic times is shown by limestone beaches at Arnside and Silverdale. The small calcareous tarn of Hawes Water below Red Bridge lane and Gaitbarrow wood is a state reserve (of 20 acres) because of its peculiar pre-glacial shell marl deposits, its freshwater molluscs and its rich flora of stoneworts.

The alternating millstone grit, sandstone, shale and coal-seams, especially in west Cumberland, also date from the Carboniferous age, which ended in coal-forests and swamps, when ferns reached the peak of their evolution. Coal-measures may be covered with up to 186ft of glacial deposit. The descending succession in Cumberland is 600ft of the Whitehaven Triassic sandstone series, with *Spirorbis* seashell-limestones and many plant remains; 1,200ft of productive middle coal-measures south of the River Derwent, correlated by its plant remains with the Midland Province; and then the lower coal-measures. Several thin coal-seams around 5ft thick have been worked in the Lower Carboniferous. The Triassic Carlisle Basin Secondary formation has some concealed upper coal-measures, and there is coal under the Cumbrian Sea Trias south of Whitehaven, but only low-gravity oil in one area of the Solway Firth's sedimentary rocks. Numerous faults dislocate the Cumbrian coalfield from north-west to south-east and pass under the southern sandstone.

Half a mile west of Humphrey Head, a low rock of red conglomerate called the Red Pinnel is attributed to Permian times, the most recent of this Palaeozoic era. Carboniferous swamps dried up in a hot Permian desert, leaving the anhydrine salt mined at Whitehaven, Walney and Penrith. Then, 200 million years ago, came the shale and unfossiliferous New Red Sandstones that lie along the coast from Whitehaven to Walney, beneath Morecambe Bay from Rampside to Newbiggin and Holker, and beneath the Solway. Finally came the Ice Ages of Pleistocene times, 1 million years ago, when an icefield spread from Scandinavia and glaciers decapitated the mountains and deepened the valleys. The effect of glaciation is almost everywhere apparent in over-deepened valleys, long valley lakes and upland tarns and corries.

Immediately after the last Ice Age, about 14,000 years ago, Lakeland was a cold tundra inhabited by ptarmigan and lynx, reindeer, arctic lemming and willow grouse. Plants gradually recolonised the lower levels, and, as the climate grew warmer, gorse climbed to 2,000ft. Birch covered the lower slopes, hazel filled the valleys, and alder and willow spread throughout the swamps, where wildfowl and waders thrived. Unable to compete with newcomers from Europe now growing in the comfortable lowlands, alpine plants clung to their rigorous outposts on the cool north-facing mountain ledges, or the seaside rocks. Finally came the Flemish introduction of sheep-grazing to the

Pennines, which prevented the regrowth of many edible plants while distributing in sheep droppings the seeds of plants like lady's mantle.

Minerals

Lakeland is also rich in interesting minerals, which attract amateur rock-collectors as well as mining geologists. Many were deposited during the cooling of the granites of Eskdale and elsewhere. Among the new minerals that W. F. Davidson of Penrith found in Caldbeck Fells in 1957 was rosasite, and a pale blue-green zinc carbonate was found in old mining dumps at Roughtongill and elsewhere, along with smithsonite (zinc carbonate), hemimorphite (zinc silicate) and malachite (copper carbonate).

Zinc and lead are to be found in Skiddaw and Helvellyn. Carrock Fell has wolfram, jabbro and slate. The granite of Eskdale holds such mineral ores as lead, zinc, copper, gold and silver, which were once worked with the Neolithic 'greenstone' axes, whose makers had manufacturing sites at Langdale Pikes, Scafell Pike and Borrowdale, and traded them with southern England. Where the deepest perma-frost action of the Ice Ages opened up 30ft fractures in the volcanic rocks under the boulder clay on the north side of Wet Sleddale, grey sections of Borrowdale volcanic, cut by intruding Shap granite, show pinkish quartz porphyry and dikes of felspar. Granite is not very common in Lakeland, except round the foot of Wastwater, east to Burnmoor Tarn and Hard Knott, south to the coastal fells near Bootle and northwards to Ennerdale and Buttermere. Its felspar is tinged with red.

Commercial salt below the Keuper marl and glacial clay at Barrow and Walney is probably of the same geological age as Cheshire salt, and that pumped at Stalmine in west Lancashire. Old copper mines linger from Keswick to Coniston and Warton Crag. It is interesting, as in Merioneth, to notice plants, even calcicoles, tolerating copper, and others tolerating lead sites.

Fluorspar, fairly rare in Lakeland, was found in old Brandelhow lead mine near Catbells.

Small quantities of gold sent people prospecting in 1970 to old mine-workings in Mungrisdale, above Troutbeck. Alluvial gold is found from time to time in Lakeland, small quantities being washed occasionally down the Caldew, for instance. There are many old workings of silver-rich lead and tungsten where small quantities of gold have been found. Silver was found in the Sand Mines on Dunfell.

Galena, the grey ore of lead (lead sulphide), was mined on Alston Moor, and England's highest road was built for the mine at Hartside—1,910ft. Higher still at Killhope Cross—2,056ft—by the Alston–Stanhope road is a fine view of the Eden Valley, where lead was also worked on Pennine escarpments. Alston's gravelly area of ancient shallow pits, an old ore-sifting site, was probably medieval. Galena was also worked above Hilton on Scordale, at Great Rundale above Dufton (near Temple Sowerby), at Keswick, Cross Fell and the Greenside valley below Sticks Pass (near Patterdale). Small hill-reservoirs were sometimes built for the lead industry, as on the fell above Hilton, or natural tarns were adapted. Lead and zinc are to be found in the Skiddaw and Helvellyn areas. Quite a different mineral appears in the igneous rocks of Borrowdale and Dove Dale in the graphite or blacklead, the 'wad' of old Keswick pencils.

Smelting the iron ore of Furness led to coppicing the lower hills with hazel, willow, oak, alder, etc, as far as Grizedale. Iron ore was also worked at Workington, Bowness Knott, and Ennerdale—commemorated at the last named in Iron Crag on Reveline, the long mountain south of the lake, and in the River Ehen (the iron river), which was stained ochre by the ore. Another site was Hodbarrow Hollow, Millom, the lowest part of Cumberland, by the Duddon estuary. Zinc was mined with fluorspar at Nanthead, above Alston. Syenite forces itself into view between Buttermere and the south end of Ennerdale (where it is pink), and on parts of High Stile. Another igneous rock to be found at Buttermere is granophyre. Greenstone, which marks parts of the

Derwent bed, is quarried at Sproutcragg in Great Langdale. There are gypsum deposits in the seabed off St Bees. One of Britain's major deposits of barytes (barium sulphate) is the Silverband mine 2,300ft high in the Westmorland Pennines, which tunnels under Great Dun Fell on the Cumberland border, above the Eden Valley. Britain's highest mine, reopened in 1939, it has barium sulphate in association with galena, calcite, fluorite and quartz.

Fossils

Lakeland's oldest fossils, from ancient sea mud, lie in the black shales of the screes below the Bishop of Barf stone, near Braithwaite beside Bassenthwaite. There are also fossils in Skiddaw slate. The soft fells of Coniston limestone reveal trilobites and graptolites, which lived in the shallow sea, while shales in the Cumberland coalfield reveal univalve mussel-like shells, and fishes. Wilfrid Jackson, during peat-cutting among the postglacial shell-marl deposits at Hawes Water (Silverdale), and Burton and Yealand Mosses to the east, identified the still common *Limnea pereger* pondsnail, which was dominant in Neolithic times, along with *L. truncatula, Hygromia rufescens, H. hispida, H. liberta, Vitrea cellaria, Bithynia tentaculata, Valvata piscinalis* and *Piscidium obtusale*. Some of these, such as *Bithynia*, indicate good supplies of oxygen, lime, phosphate and algal plankton in those ancient pools.

Most interesting are the more recent mammalian remains like the Pleistocene great fallow deer or Irish 'elk' at Ravensbarrow, Hole of Horcum and Wastwater, the teeth of pine martens in the limestone fissures of Helsfell and Kendal, and the bones of birds and beasts in Dog Holes cave, 150–200ft up the west side of Warton Crag. These discoveries are much more important than the unsubstantiated myths about the last wolf speared at Humphrey Head, and the last boar hunted down near Wraysholme Tower at Cartmel or on Wild Boar Fell in the fifteenth century, even if a tusk was found in a tomb at Kirkby Stephen.

Upper Pleistocene bones of house martin, blue tit and whin-chat were found in Dog Holes cave, where the Romano-British surface layer contained a weaving comb made of deer antler. Deep down in the earth, below the Late Neolithic or Early Bronze layers, were bones of the Celtic shorthorn wild ox, the giant Irish deer, reindeer, arctic and Scandinavian lemmings, northern and Siberian voles (from the tundra fauna at the end of the great Ice Age), and many land shells, including at least one alpine-arctic (*Pyramidula ruderata*). There were also the bones of hedgehog, mole, common shrew, pygmy shrew, Daubenton's and lesser horseshoe-bats, mountain hare, bank, field and water voles, long-tailed woodmouse, weasel and badger, plus fallow and roe antlers, and the jawbones of wolf and wild boar—all normal Romano-British animals. But the exciting discoveries were from the Pleistocene series. The entrance, a 13ft vertical drop from the limestone pavement, was walled up in 1913.

Badger Hole, a small rock shelter or cave 25ft from the top of Barrow Scout, 300yd south-west of Dog Holes and 50ft from the Silverdale Road, contained cockle and mussel as well as land shells, a red deer's tine, the bones of several birds, and a pine marten's jawbone. This had seen human occupation. Fairy Hole, further below the limestone terraces, had badger remains as well as flint flakes.

Skulls of the brown bear, here from glacial to historic times, were found in caves at Heathwaite near Arnside, Whitbarrow, and together with the remains of a wolf at Halsfell near Kendal. Further wolf remains suggested a wolf den at Haverbrack Bank, Dallam Towers, where cockleshells were also found beneath Tudor pottery, and the bones of a cat and a hedgehog (a local animal since Late Neolithic times). A Roman or Bronze Age cave at Kirkhead Hill, 2 miles west of Grange near Allithwaite, contained the bones of a wild grey goose, among numerous bird bones, and those of red deer and roe, fox, badger, boar, water vole, wild cat and domestic animals probably dating from the late first century AD. Boar tusks were unearthed from the foundations of houses at Castlehead, near Grange.

Human and animal remains were also discovered in Capes Head limestone cave at Holker, and those of the small ox, wolf, badger, boar, red and roe deer, and wild cat at Merlewood, near Grange. Amateur potholers or cave-diggers discovering such bones should take care not to disturb the layers of earth, by which they are dated. New caves are most likely to be found when rocks have to be opened up to release trapped terriers put down to foxes. Large caves are usually the roosting places of bats, and, at Grange-over-Sands, Warton Crag, Boot and Edenhall, of the large cave-spider *Meta menarda*, which hangs silk egg-cocoons like pigeons' eggs. These spiders may be driven away by amateur explorers. Most caves have a modern layer of top soil that has to be removed to reach layers containing bones. Falls of rock in the past, or filling with earth, may have hidden former caves from open view. The earth has to be sifted and fingered for small bone-fragments of birds and small mammals, which are much commoner than impressive skulls and skeletons. Water-shaped avenas and bone-chambers may lie a long way from the entrance: at Dog Holes the productive areas lay many yards along narrow side-passages.

Old quarries may become the haunt of rare ferns, as at Meathop and Plumpton, the nesting refuge of ravens as Hodge Close (Oxen Fell) or the roost of jackdaws, like Silverdale (also the haunt of fly and red helleborine orchids).

Plant life of the past is seen in the stumps of native trees in the 'submerged' forests along the shores of Solway and Drigg; and in the pollen identified from the peat 'mosses' (lowland moors) at Witherslack and in Leighton and Storrs mosses at Silverdale, which reveals that post-glacial trees included birch, pine, elm, oak, lime, alder and hazel, with bracken and bog-myrtle; radio-active carbon tests date these at Silverdale's mosses and in the coal-measures to 4,000 BC. Frondlike seedbearing Palaeozoic 'ferns' of the genus *Pecopteris* such as *Cordaites principalis*, appear in the fossil flora of the main coal band here. Mining geologists use these plant fossils to indicate the age of the mining depths, as they do with fossil shells like *Carbonicola*.

The flora of the Cumberland main-band coal south of the Derwent comprises the tree-horsetails such as *Calamites varians,* *C. suckowi* and *C. cisti*; also the tree-clubmoss *Lepidodendron wortheni,* and others such as the pillar-like *Sigillaria larvigata.* The lower part of the Whitehaven coal series, which is poor in ferns, includes such tree-horsetails as *Calamites approximatus* and *C. varians,* from the Carboniferous forest, along with *Calamocadus equisetiformis, Annularia sphenophyllodes* and many others testifying to the luxury of its ancient swamps.

The peat deposits, particularly on the Pennines, reveal remains of seeds, pollen and tree-trunks from the prehistoric flora. Wing-cases of foliage-feeding aquatic beetles like *Donacia sericea* and ground-beetles like *Harpalus,* etc, are common 6ft down in the peat at Nine Standards and elsewhere, along with seeds of creeping buttercup and dodder, these remains being as old as the peat they are found in. Pollen analyses reveal a very consistent pattern of vegetation changes. Peat began to form on the Pennines about 7,000 years ago, increasing in the Late Bronze Age, until cooler, wetter conditions about 500 BC increased it further, though some erosion had begun, and with peat-cutting cottongrass sedge began to increase at the expense of sphagnum moss.

Soil

Finally, we come to the cloddy soil, the sands and the peat, ranging from the red ploughland at Penrith to the clay paths, slippery in wet weather, around the Arnside hills. In his study of the shell-marl deposits in the Silverdale–Arnside area, Jackson found evidence that after the widespread land submergence indicated by the alluvium deposited in the upper river valleys of Keer and Gilpin, and by the limestone beaches at the foot of the abrupt cliffs on the shore in early Neolithic time, a rise of land-level followed, probably in the later Neolithic, allowing the formation of peat over the old Leighton–Storrs Moss estuary and the accumulation of salt-marshes overlying the tidal silt on Silverdale shore. Peat-cutting has declined on the raised peat bog

Page 35 (right) A high seat deer-watching hide in the trees on Scaife Heights; (below) a red stag in velvet

Page 36 (above) A whiskered bat with an identity tag clipped to its wing; (left) a long-eared bat returns to its unusual upright position on the rock face after being tagged outside its cave at 1,000ft

of the Solway submerged forest at Glasson. Lakeland has many wet cotton-grass blanket-bogs on high-level areas, with peat 3–15ft deep, and drier raised bogs or mosses in the peaty margins of former lakes, rich in calcifuge plants and often nesting curlews. An old peat forest-bed lies submerged off the coast at Drigg, and the remains of fir trees are often washed up by storms.

Foulshaw Moss, in the Kent estuary, is undershot by 20–150ft of sticky clay, covered by tidal sand on the east and by up to 15ft of peat on the west, formerly overgrown with birch. The primitive lagoons here were first drained to permit peat-cutting at Nether Leven. Meathop Park's 340 acre marsh is much like east Foulshaw, and sheltered by nearby wooded hills. The modern agricultural change from ploughing to dairy farming increased and improved the grassland with fertilisers. This not only made a greener landscape, but attracted the wintering flocks of greylag geese. Much land was successfully reclaimed here in World War II.

Lord's Plain, on the opposite (Levens) estate, is black silt soil on blue clay, little above sea-level and frequently flooded, for the sluice gate against Meathop, which automatically closes as the tide comes in, only keeps back the sea. It allows a big head of fresh water to build up if the river is running high. This marshland sheep-grazing is drained by 3½ miles of ditches, in an ancient double-level system of drainage. All this, however, may be changed when Morecambe Bay is converted to a barrage or to storage reservoirs.

The coastal sands are mostly quartz, those on Walney including rock from the Scottish coast. The sands on the shores of Windermere contain volcanic fragments from Borrowdale rocks as well as quartz, felspar and occasionally little garnets. The sands of Fleswick Bay, below St Bees, are worth sifting for the scarcer rocks. There are dunes at Allonby, Drigg and Dalton-in-Furness (Roanhead), associated with a characteristic flora and fauna, especially when stabilised by marram grass, sea-couch and the more glaucous sea lyme-grass, with damper hollows between the hills.

C

CHAPTER THREE

Lakes and Tarns

CLAIFE HEIGHTS, IN the forest above Ferry House, and Fins-thwaite Tower, beyond Newby Bridge on Windermere give one a bird's-eye view of Windermere's restful scene. The lake is $10\frac{1}{2}$ miles long, England's longest and deepest, and until the recent boundary changes three-quarters of its shores were in Lancashire but all its waters in Westmorland. It is the alma mater of British freshwater biology, augmented by shallow and richer waters at Esthwaite and Elterwater.

The Lakeland region has about sixty lakes and tarns, thirteen of them over 1 mile long. The summit of Place Fell, above Patterdale, gives an eagle's view of Ullswater, the second longest lake in England, $7\frac{1}{2}$ miles of pikeless, swanless and now presumably charless, water. Other fine views of it may be had from Hallin Fell or the crag at Sandwick above Howtown, the end of the motorists' road down its east bank; on rare occasions a stag may be seen swimming across. Another large lake is Coniston Water: devoted Ruskinians should know that the best view down its $5\frac{1}{4}$ miles, the Norse Thurston Water, is from the lawn at Monk Coniston Hall, the head of this high, cold, formerly Lancashire lake. Bassenthwaite lake has four comparatively shallow and boggy miles attractive to wildfowl between Thornthwaite Forest and Skiddaw, but they are surrounded by private shores except at Ouse Bridge.

Thirlmere, $3\frac{5}{8}$ miles of rippling water 533ft above sea-level beside the A591 to Keswick, is shut off from the road by trees and the best view is from the brink of the fell across the moors

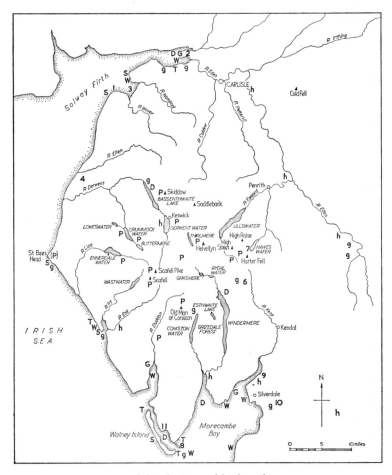

Fig 3   Bird distribution and birdwatching areas

1. Grune Point (autumn)
2. Rockliffe Marsh (autumn–winter)
3. Moricambe Bay (winter)
4. Siddick and St Helens Colliery pools (winter)
5. Drigg Point (summer)
6. Kentmere–Long Sleddale (summer)
7. Mardale–Riggindale (summer)
8. Foulney Island (summer)
9. Dallam Tower Heronry
10. Leighton Hall Moss

11. Cavendish Dock, Barrow

D. Duck (winter)
g. Gulleries
G. Geese (winter)
h. Heronries
P. Some post-war Peregrine eyries
S. Sea-bird watch (west winds)
T. Terneries (summer)
W. Wader flocks, high tide (autumn)

from Watendlath, where the buzzard circles, or from Blea Tarn at the foot of the climb up Helvellyn from Wythburn church. The lake contains 8 million gallons of trout, perch and pike water and the surrounding timber is the haunt of deer and woodcock. The forest was planted by Manchester Corporation between 1910 and 1925, mature trees being felled annually and the vacant areas replanted.

Keswick's scarred and littered Friar's Crag is a poor trippers' introduction to Derwentwater, a lake fed by eight tarns and dotted with islets where wild duck and greylag geese breed. Wastwater and Crummock should be mentioned in any brief review of the more spectacular lakes, and probably most beautiful of all (from Angler's Tarn) is Ennerdale, formerly called Broadwater and up to 148ft deep. Buttermere, famous for the pines at its head, the $1\frac{1}{2}$ miles of Loweswater, where black-necked grebes nested at one time, Grasmere's 1 mile (Anglo-Saxon Grismere, the Vale of the Wolf), and the smaller Brotherswater, can be utterly peaceful once the summer crowds have gone home, when they are left to the ubiquitous coot, the diving pochard and tufted duck.

Occupying depressions cut by glaciers and dammed by moraines, most of the lakes are too steep-sided and lack sufficient food on their pebbly shores to attract a great variety of wildfowl until frost drives them from frozen hill tarns. Wild swans winter on them, and we have seen goldeneye tarrying on Coniston until June. Shallow waters like Esthwaite and Elterwater are richest in aquatic life. Esthwaite and Windermere have altered most since the Ice Ages formed them while Ennerdale and Wastwater remain most primitive. They are rich in freshwater flatworms, of which the Lakes have nine out of the ten British species.

The highest tarn, Broad Crag on Scafell Pike, is 3,746ft above sea-level. Blea Tarn, beyond Dungeon Ghyll and the scene of the farm in Wordsworth's 'Solitary', is a summer motorists' picnic spot. Tarn Hows or Highlow Tarn with its pine trees above Coniston (not to be confused with Tarn House Tarn, a winter wildfowl haunt near Kirkby Stephen) is a bedlam of cars on sunny Sundays, though it attracts occasional whoopers and pochard when picnic cars are out of season, and greylags and mergansers nest there.

Several tarns, like Wet Sleddale and Lever's Water, became industrial reservoirs. Most of them have diatomaceous deposits. Those in the old tarn at Kentmere were worked, and the increase of diatoms such as *Asterionella formosa* at the north end of Windermere was found to follow the increased sewage from new houses built after the coming of the railway. The crustacean 'water hog-louse' *Asellus aquaticus* has so increased in half a dozen lakes that one has found it come through the tap in Coniston drinking-water, probably encouraged by algal growth in the mains. *A. meridanus* was formerly recorded as the commoner species. In June pairs of teal and mallard may occupy the wild tarn covered with floating pondweed at the top of Grizedale Forest, near the fire-watch tower, having largely deserted the public Juniper Tarn lower down, beside the forest road.

Overwater Tarn, source of the River Ellen, is rich in pike and perch ('bass' from its bars). Across the Cartmel hills from Wood Broughton one finds red-breasted mergansers nesting on Bigland Tarn, and Whinn's Tarn in the fells above Edenhall heronry has pike, perch and carp as well as (now fewer) goosanders, whoopers and other wildfowl. Goosanders come and go as the fish stocks vary, as do great crested grebes. Fisher Tarn is another interesting south-eastern water. Sunbiggin Tarn, below the *Selaginella* clubmoss at Orton Moor, between Tebay and Kirkby Stephen, is Britain's highest haunt of the sedge *Cladium mariscus*, which grows with bog-rush and slender and common spike-rushes, and also of the freshwater shrimp *lacustris*, confined to small lakes, which is food for its trout. It grows in other tarns like Cunswick. Thurstonfield (Thrussenfield) Loch, near Carlisle, now drained, was a mere 30 acres, yet one saw a variety of duck there in winter; roebuck may be seen nearby at daybreak. Even the pond in Upperby Park in Carlisle at one time attracted a regular wintering flock of pochard.

Birds

The lakes radiate from the Borrowdale–Langdale area, most with a single river, flowing out through a dammed-up barrier of morraine-drift. Twice as many duck winter on the northern lakes influenced by the Solway as on the southern waters influenced by Morecambe Bay (where the average is 500). Most of the duck favour the bays, though Killington reservoir, above Kendal, is a good haunt of mallard, teal, and wigeon, and Wyndham Mere is another near Kirkby Lonsdale. Wigeon more often use the lowland northern tarns inland from the Solway, such as Monkshill Loch, Moorhouse and the floods round Moricambe. Teal and shoveler nest there; gadwall, pintail and wigeon have also bred; and escaped duck have come from Netherby, the once-famous Border game estate near Longtown. Pennington reservoir in Furness, and Talkin and Tindale Tarns with pike and perch in the north-east and Wyndham Mere in the south-east near the B6254 are worth visiting also.

A climb up to Seathwaite Tarn, set in a rocky bowl on the west side of Coniston Old Man at the top of Dunnerdale, is often not rewarding ornithologically; once I just found a pair of sandpipers nesting—and nor are visits to Ullswater (except for an osprey carrying nesting material to a wood without building in 1970), Buttermere and Thirlmere. Cold Coniston Water attracts winter whoopers, summer mergansers, sandpipers and migrating autumn swallows, and occasionally dipper and grey wagtail may be found feeding round its pebbly shores. Fir Island, on its eastern side, is the favoured haunt of cormorants.

Elterwater's old Norse name, Elpt Vatn, meant swan lake. Herds of up to twenty-seven whoopers visit it in winter with diving duck and Slavonian grebe. A belief that wild swans arrive first there is not true; but whoopers first appeared in the 1951–2 winter early in November, moving later to Little Langdale and Loughrigg Tarns and on to Rydal Water, Esthwaite and Grasmere, Barngates Tarn (Hawkshead) and other waters. I recorded the increasing visits of whoopers from November to

May in the early 1950s. Up to forty have been seen displaying and trumpeting on Grasmere. They return to Rydal, Blelham Tarn, Bowness Bay and Waterhead. At St Helens colliery pond near the Maryport–Workington road, I saw in December 1968 a rare visitor, the little bunting (this corner of Lakeland once had a cream-coloured courser and a Wilson's petrel from the southern hemisphere at Allonby, though the latter was not fully confirmed) and some whoopers among a herd of mute swans, with tufted duck and goldeneye, in the midst of industry. At Keswick next day more whoopers were on Derwentwater, where a raft of wild duck rode the leeward side of Lord's Island in a gale, goldeneye dived for food and a long line of cormorants flew up the lake.

When the high tarns freeze, coot descend to the larger unfrozen lakes; 250 tufted duck with 700 coot, plus goldeneye, have been counted on Windermere between Storrs and Waterhead Bay, at Rampholme and Ferry Nab, and also Millersground Bay at Bowness. In winter the little black-necked grebe has visited Blakeholme at the southern end of the lake; 272 goldeneye were on it in January 1972. Wild greylags occasionally rest at Bassenthwaite's reedy Bowness Bay on their way overland from Solway, via Dunmail Raise, to winter on Meathop Marsh, opposite Arnside. Three Greenland whitefronts were here on one occasion. Winter bitterns sometimes visit the Bassenthwaite reeds too, and remain there to boom (see Chapter Nine), possibly nesting in 1972. A score of goldeneye often dive in Scarness Bay and 40 tufted duck in Broadness Bay in winter, and shelduck sometimes rest there. Yet when few duck were no Bassenthwaite one February, Derwentwater had a raft of 90 pochard as well as 10 goosanders in view from the road below Cat Bells, and goosanders, whoopers, Canada geese and tufted duck opposite Derwent Bank.

About 200 pochard and tufted duck winter on Derwentwater and Bassenthwaite. Even Rydal and Grasmere are visited. Some 200 mallard are Hawes Water's chief winter birds. Over 40 greylags and as many tufted duck flock to Esthwaite in winter. More interesting, however, has been the post-war colonisation of the Lakes by breeding mergansers. In June 1961 a pair of red-breasted mergansers occupied the Bowness end of Windermere and next summer a pair nested on the east side of Coniston Water, near Thurston-Brantwood, with a pair of pied flycatchers in a tree not far away. Such was the increase in the now ubiquitous mergansers that, despite speedboats, I saw a flock of 11 on this lake in June 1970. This success story began with the red-breasted mergansers' increase in Scotland, whence they extended their breeding range via the Border Esk to the arm of another Esk, opposite Ravenglass on the coast in 1950. Then they moved to the island gullery on Stocks Reservoir at Slaidburn Dalehead in 1957, since when the species has steadily increased, to occupy almost all waters with increasing tameness. The birds were nesting on Crummock in 1967, then Ullswater, and in 1971 four pairs nested in the Windermere woods north of Ferry House and three pairs near Lakeside at the south. At the same time, they went on to colonise north-west Yorkshire and Wales. By contrast, the increase of the goosander has so far stopped in Lakeland, where it nests mostly by rivers.

The recording of wildfowl is considerably confused by widespread introductions of feral greylag geese, barnacles, European whitefronts, forest beans, pinkfeet, Canada geese, even gadwall in Westmorland, as well as Carolina wood-duck. From 1961 Scottish greylags were introduced to Hawes marsh at the Duddon estuary, and elsewhere. Subsequently they began nesting across Lakeland from the Kentmere reservoir above Kendal to islands on Derwentwater, Crummock, Grizedale Forest Tarn, Devoke Water, Rydal, Tarn Hows and Ravenglass. Up to 40 now visit Esthwaite Water. Some return in winter to the Duddon and some, crossing the Solway in summer, may be developing a moult-migration to less disturbed haunts of feral Wigtownshire birds at Lochinch, near Stranraer. A similar moult-migration brings mute swans from the Midlands and Oxford to Barrow's huge Cavendish Dock (though a mute swan ringed in Lithuania was traced to the Solway), and of shelduck from north

Morecambe Bay and Solway across the Pennines to the German coast. Lakeland's winter goosanders may fly via Stocks Reservoir and Coniston Cold (in the Yorkshire Pennines) to the Staffordshire–Midland reservoirs and even to the London reservoirs. Pinkfeet and greylags fly over Windermere in spring and autumn, travelling between Morecambe Bay and the Solway Firth; and 272 goldeneye were on Windermere in January 1972.

Great crested grebes nest on many lakes, such as Esthwaite, Coniston Water and Blelham, but not shallow Leighton Moss (though one visited it in July 1972). Their numbers depend on the stocks of fish in various waters, and, like many birds, they recover quickly from the losses in severe winters. They take newts, frogs and tadpoles as well as fish. Because many fish rise nearer the surface at night, grebes will fish after dark on moon-lit nights or early in the morning. A pair will eat about 300lb of food a year, but many winter along the sea coast or in mild Morecambe Bay. Coot are their chief competitors for nesting territory.

Mallard nest in many places, teal and tufted duck (27 sites) use a few reedy waters (the latter on Esthwaite and Blelham), pochard have 10 sites, and a few shelduck nest in the wooded banks of Windermere and Coniston. The late H. A. Fooks had regular wild shelduck visitors at his home, now a memorial deer museum, at Haybridge in the old Lancashire fells between Bouth and Satterthwaite. Shoveler have 9 nesting sites in the south and north-west, wigeon have bred in 4 or 5 Pennine sites on the south-eastern moors, and sandpipers nest on the shores of most lakes. Black-headed gulls occupy or occupied Low Oxen Fell tarn where I saw nests with young in 1972, above Langdale Tarn, Lowick Common, 5 miles north of Ulverston, Beacon Tarn, Roerigg Tarn and a score of other places, moving when disturbed by humans, or when low water permits fox-predation. These gulls add their noise to Leighton Moss, and between 1,000 and 3,000 fly over the fells at dusk to roost in winter on the marsh near Windermere's Millersground Bay.

Spring and autumn migrants include black terns, brought on

east winds; in August 1959 the largest British tern, the Caspian, appeared at Windermere and the end of July 1966 saw another at Leighton Moss. Occasional Slavonian grebes have been seen on Grasmere and Windermere's Rayrigg Bay in January, with 40 pochard (twice as many on Rydal) and a dozen goldeneye. Cormorants roost in winter on Roughholme and Ladyholme islands near Bowness on Windermere, when large numbers of woodpigeons roost in the woods at Wray. Cormorants ringed on Farne have been recovered on Windermere, and a heron from Belgium was recovered at Crofton, Cumberland. Most of the wintering black-headed gulls are immature Baltic birds, rather than those from Lakeland gulleries at Bassenthwaite or various tarns. One winter I watched a red-throated diver for weeks on a small deep field-pond at Botcherby, outside Carlisle, where it often rested out on the bank, though these birds are only supposed to come ashore to nest.

Fish

Anglers from flatter counties will find no carp or bream and few tench in the Lake District. Pike and perch dominate the level lakes. A few salmon climb the rivers, but very few reach Ennerdale; they spawn in Rydal, Grasmere and rarely the becks in Windermere. Sea trout (a migratory form of brown trout, not a separate species) run into Bassenthwaite, Windermere, Derwentwater and Crummock and reach High Fell, Greendale and Scoats Tarns above Wastwater. Roach inhabit Esthwaite and Rydal Waters, and Skelsmergh Tarn near Kendal. Whinfell Tarn contains large rudd, perch, pike and chub (confusingly called 'skelly', a different fish), which were introduced to upper Ullswater, a practice as confusing to recorders of distribution as introducing waterfowl. Indian grass-carp were introduced into the warm water of the almost disused Cavendish Dock at Barrow in an attempt to cope with its growth of weed. Burnmoor Tarn on Eskdale Fell has pike as well as trout, Hayes Water (Penrith) and Easedale and Codale Tarns near Grasmere have perch and trout, while Ulverston's Canal Foot augmented the coarse fish with common carp, roach, perch, eels and gudgeon. Mockerin Tarn near Loweswater has pike and perch, as has lonely Overwater, above Keswick.

Minnows compete for food with young perch and trout, and elvers in the Leven hunt the same midge larvae as do trout. Yellow-bellied female eels may live as long as seventeen years in the lakes, feeding on small shellfish, freshwater shrimps and caddis-creepers, and further competing with salmon and trout for most small fish, though the number of char and trout eggs and salmon-fry they eat is not considered significant. A 9lb eel was taken from Windermere. A distribution map of the three-spined stickleback published to boost the 10sq km recording scheme in 1970 was obviously incomplete, with records only from Windermere and Ennerdale becks. Grasmere holds trout, perch, pike (once 28lb) and eels. Coniston Water's trout, perch and pike are free-fishing like those in Windermere, Derwentwater and Bassenthwaite providing one has a river authority licence. Bitterling were liberated in Esthwaite, Rydal, Grasmere.

Absent from Ennerdale and Ullswater, pike are the chief winter predators upon trout and, where they exist, char in lakes like Esthwaite, Rydal and Windermere, where over 8,000 were netted in 1944 (and some 300 over 3lb were taken annually at one period), to help increase char. Their numbers do not alter much. Most are four years old, and several females (which grow faster and larger than males—anglers' weight-records too often ignore sex) reach fourteen years. The oldest caught was seventeen, and the biggest, a 35¼lb female, was fourteen years old. Male pike rarely exceed 12lb. They favour the sheltered centre and bays of Windermere, not the deeper parts, and travel little, except to cross from one side of the lake to the other, the females spawning annually in the same reedbeds in early spring. There is more substance in the tales of the ancient 'monster' of Mordern Mere, a dark Cumbrian tarn and a noted pike water, than in those of the Loch Ness monster. Richard Walkyre's fifteenth-century 'vast fysshe of Morderyne Meere' was one more pike that got away.

Windermere, which has salmon, trout, char, pike, perch, eel, roach, rudd, stone-loach, bullhead, minnow, tench and three-spined stickleback, became famous for the short-lived World War II canning (at Leeds) of its bony perch, trapped in the north and south basins. The biggest weighed 3¼lb, though anglers, who catch most at Millersground, near the entrance of Wynlass Beck into the lake, have caught perch up to 4lb (1963). One wartime perch-trap caught 350 toads, and several took eels and pike. Most Windermere perch are eight years old, and some reach ten years. Mature fish of two years (male) and three years (female) and over make a spring inshore migration to spawn in 5–20ft from mid-May to mid-June. Marked perch, taken in successive years in the same spawning trap, show a territorial breeding memory typical of so many more animals than just the homing birds. Large numbers of fry appear later in these shallows, and big trout as well as pike prey upon them. As young perch feed on different plankton species, they do not compete with plankton-feeding char. Autumn sees a migration back to deeper winter haunts, where young fish feed on bottom insects. A man caught 137 perch fishing in the evening at Windermere in August 1927.

To guddle (fish) for trout is the chief interest of Lakeland anglers (the char and trout season being 3 March to 30 September). Windermere, which also has Loch Leven trout, has brown trout weighing 6 and 7lb. Big bull trout were once acclaimed as a separate species, *Salmo ferox*, with a rounder tail (often clipped and sold as salmon in wartime), as were 'Ullswater trout'. The latter also inhabit Wastwater, Ennerdale and Crummock, where they have reached 14lb; an old Patterdale boatman claimed a 16½lb trout from Ullswater in 1926, but it was not caught by angling. Most trout are caught by spinning and trolling, until the mayfly hatch in June. Winds are often variable and of enough force on Windermere to spoil roadside fishing for the 1–3lb trout. Its trout have reached 12lb, and Ennerdale produced an 8lb specimen in 1920 and has reached 7lb since, its average being ¾lb. Derwentwater is noted for its red trout, and like Bassenthwaite it also has perch, pike, salmon and char. Rainbow trout (American steelhead trout) have been introduced to waters like Lupton Reservoir near Kendal.

More interesting to the naturalist is Lakeland char (*Salvelinus alpinus*) landlocked after the Ice Ages in the cold deep lakes to which it had migrated from northern seas to spawn. Local varieties or geographical subspecies include Willoughby's Windermere char (*S. a. willoughbii*), the largest of Lakeland char, which also inhabits Coniston Water, Crummock, Ennerdale, Buttermere (with pike and perch), Wastwater, Goatswater and Seathwaite Tarn, and is the food of eels, goldeneye and other diving duck. Introductions to Loweswater, Bassenthwaite and Derwentwater failed, for these lakes are too shallow and warm. Ullswater, where char used to spawn in Glenridding Beck, was restocked in 1895, but seems to have lost its stock through lead poisoning from the adjacent mines. Char cannot survive in water over 59° F, so they do not inhabit shallow Grasmere, Rydal or Esthwaite. About 1870, Windermere was restocked with 180,000 reared at a hatchery on Wansfell; but efforts to introduce them into Hawes Water to increase the size of its Lonsdale char (*lonsdalii*) failed. This is a smaller race (maybe because Hawes Water's hard rocks yield little mineral food), reaching 7in and weighing 3oz, with a longer and more pointed snout, narrower operculum, smaller eyes and larger fins.

The char is the handsomest British fish, beautifully scarlet-bellied or orange-finned according to season with blue-green backs rather like mackerel, and delicious to taste. Without the trout's splash they take winged ants or, in autumn, artificial 'fly' in 'belbing' or char-fishing as they follow the evening rise of plankton, especially at Goatswater. Their fondness for cold deep lakes makes trolling the usual method of fishing for them and, until netting the spawning shoals ended on Windermere, potted char and char pie were sold in hotels. From March to September they are fished in the deeper northern and southern ends down to 80ft, with long line-trawls from a rod without reel, and droppers or tail-lines at 15ft intervals. Another method is to use a plumb- ('ploomb'-) line with a 1½lb lead at the bottom and bright metal spinners. Like trout, their size varies with their food: the largest in Windermere are 9–10in and nearly 3lb in weight, but the average is 10oz. They tend to be smaller and darker on other waters, eg about ½lb in Coniston.

Shoals feed near the bottom on aquatic insects, molluscs, crustaceans, tiny fish fry and worms. They spawn from November to February, small fish returning annually to the River Brathay (slightly colder than the Rothay) and to shallows near the banks, and larger fish preferring slightly deeper water. Some spring spawners lay in February and March in 60–80ft of water. Their eggs lie unprotected in the stones, unlike the salmon's redd, and hatch in ten weeks. Early in April the young char move into deeper cooler water. Sometimes char interbreed with trout.

Another fish landlocked in the Lakes is the whitefish, *Coregonus lavaretus*, which has the adipose or fatty rear fin of Salmonids but the deeply forked tail, large nocturnal eyes, larger silvery scales and planktonic diet of herrings. As with char, variation arose among isolated breeding stocks. Whitefish are curiously absent from Windermere and Coniston, probably because they reached their lakes from Solway via the Eden, not from Morecambe Bay like some of the char. They are less numerous than char and only exceptionally take crusts in Derwentwater and Bassenthwaite, where they are called vendace (*C. l. gracilior*). They are more slender, shorter-finned and shorter-headed than Scottish specimens and reach a length of 9in. In Hawes Water, Ullswater (Gale Bay) and Red Tarn an abundant larger variety called schelly, sheely, shelly, or skelly (*vandesius*) sometimes grows just over 16in and weighs 1¼lb. On rare occasions some of these enter the Eden and its tributaries; but schelly is also a vernacular name for roach, dace and chub and 'skellie-fuddling' on the Irthing at Newby Bridge (not the southern one) is catching and burning vermin chub.

Called whitefish from their white scales, whose rings indicate their age, as in herrings, the sexes separate in winter, spawning together in the new year in gravelly inshore water, scattering eggs and milt at dusk like herrings, then migrating to deeper water before the warmth of summer. Otherwise they shoal by age-groups, feeding, as their subterminal mouth indicates, in the bottom weed upon copepods, small shellfish and insect larvae. Perch, eels and older whitefish eat their eggs.

Insects

Windermere's once famous rise of green drakes (first winged 'dun' of the mayfly) declined in inverse ratio to motorboats, even before World War II. To a lesser extent this has happened on Derwentwater, but Bassenthwaite has been spared the petrol invasion, and Ullswater has a phenomenal evening rise of mayfly that help to fill the trout-baskets. Insect life in the lakes is connected with that of the rivers, but the discovery of a new British water-beetle, *Stenelmis caniculatus*, near Ferry House in 1960 shows what opportunities Windermere still offers the naturalist. Windermere and Coniston, like the River Brathay, harbour the large caddis *Athripsodes nigroervosus*, whose creeper (nymph) is probably still unknown. The Ings or Stable Hills Fen is an interesting site opposite Lord's Island at Derwentwater.

The Lakes also have 59 out of Britain's 90 so-called water-fleas (*Cladocera*)—small freshwater copepod crustaceans.

The moorland tarns are home for the claret dun *Leptophlebia vespertina*, the small caddis *Hydroptilid* in flask-shaped cases, the water-flea *Eurycercus lamellata*, sheep-fluke pond-snails, water-boatmen, metallic blue *Lestes* dragonflies, the small red *Pyrrhosoma nymphula*, the small blue *Enallagma cyathigerum*, the great red sedge *Phryganea grandis*, *Lymnophilus* stoneflies, the deep-water olive *Cleone simile* and freshwater shrimps—as well as trout to eat them. The southern dragonfly *Aeschna cyanea* attacks the dark green fritillary butterflies on Hampsfell on hot July days. Even high tarns lure insects. Spiral vegetable-cases of the caddis-creeper *Phryganea obsoleta*, with three bands on its head, may be found in Grizedale Tarn near Helvellyn's Dollywagon Pike. Lower down its relative *veria* is found in Moss Eccles and

Bore Tree Tarns, and *striata* appears in Bore Tree as well as Windermere. Some, like the long slender spirally-pointed cases of *Triaenodes bicolor*, inhabit high and low waters, and *Molanna angustata*'s tube (with lateral extensions) is to be found in high Bore Tree and low Esthwaite. Many stream and river caddis inhabit the stony lake-shores. The rare *Limnephilus xanthodes* inhabits Blelham Bog in fair numbers.

Plants

Windermere sometimes greens with algal bloom like the Shropshire meres in autumn; herb paris, a Lakeland rarity, grows beneath its yews, and a summer walk from Ferry House to above Belle Grange finds the little reddish-yellow spotted balsam *noli-angere* seeding freely (and on the east shore of Derwentwater and at Newby Bridge, Garsdale, etc). Unspotted small yellow *parviflora* grows only on the west side of Lake Windermere. One's summer approach to Coniston beside the confluence of Crake and lake finds acres of yellow water-flags. Water lobelia was said to poison the mute swans on Ullswater but this is not listed in Scott's recent monograph on swans. Shoreweed and quillwort grow like miniature aloes on many a stony bed. Nevertheless—it is the shallow lakes that most interest the botanist.

A footpath opposite the lane from Grizedale, a short way along the road from Hawkshead, brings one to the head of Esthwaite, where bog myrtle, *Sphagnum* and *Mollinia* spread out from a stand of common sallow, and there are bog asphodel and the spotted yellow throats of American monkey-musk to admire. Here grows the wiry, brittle, pale-green submerged North American aquatic *Hydrilla lithuanica* (*Anacharis occidentalis* and *Elodea nuttallii*), whose only other British haunt is near Renvyle in Connemara. It has whorls of five narrow ½in leaves (sometimes only three or four), and often whorls of three shorter and broader leaves near the base of the shoots. It reaches a height of 16in, with the nodes between its leafings up to 1in apart, and, like

Page 53   The bird-watcher's thrill: a golden eagle showing typical horizontal wingspan and up-turned primaries

Page 54 (*left*) The falcon of the crags—a cock peregrine; (*below*) a pair of young peregrines or 'eyasses' on their nest ledge

Canadian pondweed, it does not flower or seed here, though its winter buds are prominent. It grows in about 8ft of water, with the slender naiad, which is more branched above with shorter internodes, lesser and grassy pondweeds, and autumnal star-wort. W. H. Pearsall and his son, who discovered *Hydrilla* here, suggested that migratory wildfowl brought it from its native eastern Europe; though botanists may too often attribute isolated plant-rarities to birds, migratory wildfowl visit so many lakes that it should have been spread further in the sixty years since its discovery, and it seems more likely that it was introduced by a botanist or aquarist.

The footpath enters this North Fen reserve with the Black Beck, meeting a silty vegetative succession: a fen-carr and bog develops into a sallow wood, with one of Lakeland's few well-grown haunts of reed mace, true bulrush sedge and a mixture of tufted and beaked sedges growing in inorganic sedimentation. The area is loud in summer with chattering sedge warblers and monotonously repetitive reed buntings, and the footpath finally leads to open water where great crested grebes display, sandpipers whistle, and mergansers and greylags and Canada geese may be seen.

Another good sphagnum-bog forms the north-western end of Blelham Tarn, again with bog myrtle and *Mollinia* grass, as well as white-beaked and downy sedges and the great sundew's red leaves, glistening with their viscid insect-traps. The true swamp or raft-spider here, *Dolomedes fimbriatus*, is rarely found in north-western England. Great crested and little grebes also nest at Blelham, with tufted duck.

Shoreweed and sedge, broad-leaved pondweed and water lobelia border many a moorland tarn, where one may spring teal or find summer sandpipers and black-headed gulls nesting. Lake clubrushes (*Scirpus*) are used in Ambleside church rush-bearing, in July. Quillwort in Coniston Water below Brant-wood, and in Hawes Water, is not always a mountain plant as botany books imply. Its smaller relative *echinospora* joins it at Derwentwater. Yellow globe-flowers (*Trollius*) grow among the

D

bistort in the north-east banks of Coniston Water. You will find sand leek in the banks of Windermere and saw wort, tway-blade, bog pimpernel, Solomon's seal and marsh orchids round Grasmere. Water-plantain is abundant at Windermere Lake. Ullswater's shores have the variety of lesser meadow rue known as *majus* at Pooley Bridge, yellow loosestrife, floating bur reed, etc. Water lobelia pokes its pale lilac flowers out of Derwent-water, Windermere, Rydal, Coniston and Ullswater. Despite its name, alpine enchanter's nightshade borders Ullswater, Derwentwater and Buttermere, while bogbean grows as high as at Glaramara in Cumberland. White butterbar escaped from cultivation to the Millersground end of Windermere, and the small white orchid *alba* used to grow near Windermere.

Monkey-musk was found at Howtown (Ullswater) in 1906 and is now widespread by Lakeland streams. Though the original site of the purple-dotted American yellow loosestrife *Lysimachia terrestris* at Bowness has been built upon, a large colony flourishes at the south end of Windermere, though it seldom produces red bulbils, as did the former. The American slender rush *Juncus tenuis*, found at Thirlmere in 1906, is still extending its range. Two uncommon native rushes are the mountain *J. alpinus*, found at Cumberland's East Side Tarn in 1900, and the lakeside *J. filiformis*, which grows on Coniston shore and by Esthwaite, Crummock, Derwentwater, Bassen-thwaite and Buttermere. It was exterminated from Thirlmere, however, by the reservoir. *Iris versicolor* is by Ullswater.

The aquarist may also find a wealth of pondweeds, ranging from the lesser *Potamogeton pusillus* and hornwort in lakes like Esthwaite and Windermere to the tall slender *berchtoldii*, also found in these waters and at Coniston, Derwentwater, Bassen-thwaite and Ullswater, and to the grassy *obtusifolius* in Grasmere. Less glamorous than the bog pimpernel around Elterwater or floating bur reed in the mountain tarn above Grasmere they 'furnish' the lakes, as they do our aquarium fish-tanks, with essential food and shelter for a chain of waterlife. The small tarns, however, change rapidly, and Ennerdale Lake, for instance, is one of the least hospitable waters to aquatic life. Dipper and cormorant are its most loyal birds, and it is note-worthy as England's only haunt of an uncommon freshwater shrimp, *Mysis relicta*, of marine origin, and of the tiny copepod crustacean *Limnocalanus macrurus*. Most tarns are girt with sedges —a thick sward of shoreweed filling the shallows with its bugs and beetles. Then, in open deeper water, float the broad oval leaves of *Potamogeton natans*, a resting-place for the red dragonfly *Pyrrhosoma*. The depths harbour water-milfoil, home of the caseless web-spinning caddis *Holocentropus dubius*, the free-swimming larval pond mayfly or Lake Olive, *Cleone simile*, and the blue dragonfly *Enallagma*. The spider *Aranea cornutus* is com-mon around marshy reed beds and the northern wolf-spider *Lycosa agricola* occurs by river and lake verges. Leighton Moss is one of three British haunts of the water 'flea' *Scapholeberis aurita*.

CHAPTER FOUR

Mountains

Mammals

THE ROOF OF Lakeland consists of wild crags split by dark vertical ravines, sliced through by gullies and snow-covered in winter. This is the only part of England with mountains over 3,000ft—four of them. Fifty peaks exceed 2,000ft, and there are seventeen passes of over 1,000ft. Built up by intensive volcanic activity in the Ordovician period, and worn down again in glacial times, the crags are the homes of eagle, peregrine, buzzard and raven, and the gullies belong to the ring-ouzel. Arctic alpine flowers tuck their roots in screes and ledges of volcanic ash, and, also surviving since glacial times, are alpine butterflies not found again until one reaches Switzerland.

Rocky bields (earths) are the retreat of the gaunt grey mountain foxes, the 'greyhound' foxes whose development was probably influenced by the immigration of Scandinavian *vulpes* types when the land-bridge joined Scotland to Scandinavia. Smaller lowland foxes are now replacing them. These are hunted by the little Lakeland hounds—Coniston hounds killed a white fox in 1947—but they rarely leave their home ranges, which are areas of not more than 1–2½ square miles. Young dog foxes, however, may travel many miles. Bushy-tailed pine martens use the same rocky retreats, though they may be seen in Ennerdale on winter nights. Even otters pass between high watersheds. Feral goats several times formed herds on the fells between Coniston and Tilberthwaite, and elsewhere.

Mountain hares are absent from most of Lakeland and the Pennines, except for a few on the Cumbrian border moors above Gilsland and Bewcastle. Across a high moor above Halt-whistle, where golden plover whistled in chorus far above the Eden Valley, when seeking the lovely spring dotterel in one of its last breeding haunts after Mickle Fell and Fairfield, I found that a few mountain hares, lean and lop-eared, had wandered in from the Cheviots. On this border hill, tracks and droppings led to the dry burrow of a pine marten in a bank of peat, with sheep's wool and grass for its litter. Here, as in Wales, it is adapted to a moorland life, foraging for voles, young grouse and plovers—until driven out by a vixen heavy with cubs. Field voles live as high as 1,900ft at Nethermost Cove in the Helvellyn range, moles at 2,000ft and badgers at 1,000.

Birds

Many Eagles' Crags and Ravens' Rocks testify to the richness of Lakeland bird life before stock-rearing and game-preservation destroyed the predators. Golden eagles' eyries are situated where the Rigg extends like a finger into the head of Mardale's Hawes Water and at Rainsborrow Crag above Kentmere; they begin laying at the end of March. Above the Rigg and the scattered Herdwick sheep, the ground rises steeply to the rocky Swine Crag, Heron Crag and Eagle Crag, which may be seen from the face of Harter Fell. The peregrines that came from their Long Sleddale eyrie above Kentmere to rob the Riggindale eagles at Mardale Head in 1971 brought to mind a female peregrine, now stuffed, trapped on Flake Howe Crags in 1922 and a three-year-old female golden eagle trapped on Brether-dale near Shap in 1960, with sheep's wool (perhaps carrion) in its stomach. A young eagle was recently seen in Eskdale and elsewhere. From 1947 we began seeing and recording immature golden eagles, wandering in winter from Scotland over an area from Bassenthwaite to Cartmel and roosting near Bewcastle and Hawkshead until eggs were laid in 1969 on a buttress of High Street, after a previous failure in Borrowdale. A pair frequented Skiddaw in 1970, and in July 1971 an immature eagle soared over Newby Bridge, south Windermere.

Peregrines seem to be recovering from a decline due to secondary poisoning from pesticides. They have many traditional eyries and, like eagles, usually alternate between two sites: Slape (or Slipper) Crag, above Bassenthwaite, was an alternative for a pair that nested on Dead Crag by Dash Falls. Peregrines also bred in modern times at Blue Ghyll and Frostwick, near Kirkstone Pass, Walla Crag (Derwentwater), and many other known sites; climbing drove them from some, and their deserted eyries are now often occupied by screaming kestrels. (The counties of Cumberland and Westmorland were included in a War Office instruction I still possess on sites for the destruction of 'Hawks, Peregrine Falcons', which I ignored as an Army Pigeon Service officer in World War II, though the RAF was not so lenient and by 1943 the birds were reduced to three pairs.)

Buzzards are common mountain-birds, though the postwar increase in climbing has driven them, too, from rock sites; they also fluctuate with the vole population. There are some seventy ravenages in the mountains, ranging from near Ulpha Bridge (Dunnerdale) to the top of Langdale (where for years one raven laid woodcock-red erythristic eggs) and Lambfold quarry, which one year had an unusually large clutch of seven eggs.

Above the 1,000ft juniper contour, the ring-ouzel in summer gives away its presence with its mournful whistle, and its white gorget can be picked out on most mountains. Above the Copper Mines youth hostel at the top of Coniston's Church Beck in the Furness Fells in 1970 we tracked down the territories of eight pairs on the east side of the Old Man, Lancashire's highest point; but from Ulpha Bridge up the slope to Seathwaite Tarn, the wetter western side, only three pairs.

Even in winter the wren chitters loudly in Coniston's rocky heights and the 2,635ft summit of the Old Man may be swept by swifts. Cuckoos lay their eggs in the nests of the mountain's meadow-pipits, and I have seen a cock kestrel in flight beside the Old Man strike down a pipit and strip it on a rock, like a

peregrine. Golden plover nest at 2,000ft on the Pennine side of
Lakeland, and migrating dotterel still visit level tops where they
used to nest on Fairfield, Cold Fell and Mickle Fell. A flock of
snow-buntings flew 1,500ft above Hawes Water one February
and on Cross Fell in March. Grey and pink-foot geese fly over
Dunmail Raise.

Moths and Butterflies

Entomologists need the legs of mountain goats to hunt for the
northern wave and the dark Aviemore form of the northern
dart moth on the slopes of Skiddaw and at 1,900ft at the Moor
House reserve in July. The grey mountain carpet moth is more
an insect of the high fells, and the northern eggar of Walla Crag,
above Derwentwater. Many grey carpets are on the south side
of Bowfell in July. England's only alpine butterfly, the dark-
brown orange-banded and spotted little mountain ringlet, lives
by grassy rills 1,800–2,000ft up the mountainside, sometimes
as low as 700ft; it flies close to the ground, looking almost black
on the wing, on sunny days in late June and July—not in dull
weather like the Ben Lomond race. Smaller and lighter-coloured
than the Scottish and Irish specimens, with small black dots replacing the 'eyes', the Lakeland variety was originally named
cassiope and is now *mnemon*. Its green caterpillar, with its darker
green lines and a white stripe, feeds on mat-grass, sheep's fescue
and annual meadow-grass in wet places, taking two years to
mature and pupating among the grass stems. Having evolved a
sub-species unknown on the Continent, from where it arrived
in the later part of the third Pleistocene glaciation, it is believed
to be the most ancient of British butterflies.

The Scotch argus butterfly and many moths are more typical
of the fells than of the windswept rocky heights; but the common magpie moth occurs at 2,000ft on Fairfield, the tissue moth
1,900ft up at Moor House, and the sallow kitten at Coniston. Just
as lowland woodsorrels, foxgloves, anemones, wood-sage and
so on mix with alpine plants, so one finds well above 1,000ft

on the Old Man of Coniston pond-skater and caddis-nymph in the tarns, dor-beetle and garden chafer in the turf and bracken. Even at 3,000ft in sunny June or October, migrating large and green-veined white butterflies and red admirals may be met fluttering across the mountains. The large Scandinavian ground-beetle *Carabus glabratus* is another mountaineer here, and *Carabus nitens* is found at 1,700ft on Nine Standards. Migrant butterflies are not to be associated with such mountain insects as the ground-beetles seen hunting the black slugs in the turf along the high sheep-tracks. Here leatherjackets replace earthworms.

Lady's mantle, distributed by sheep, attracts the red carpet moth. The larvae of an attractive little grass moth, *Crambus furcatellus*, probably eats the roots of sheep's fescue on Langdale Pikes and Coniston Old Man. Sheep droppings feed the larval dor-beetles, *stercorarius*, and the yellow dung-fly, *vernalis*, which in turn feed foxes. The beetle *Leistus montanus* lives on Skiddaw and elsewhere, and the predatory beetle *Diamous coerulescens* among dampy mossy rocks, probably feeding on cranefly larvae. *Theobaldia alaskaensis* is one of the rarer mosquitoes of the hills. The Linythid spider *Poeciloneta globosa* occurs at 1,000–2,000ft in Lakeland and the Pennines, and the dark *Eboria caliginosa* is known in Britain only on Scafell Pike and Marsden Moor. The mottled grey mountain spider *Leotyphantes whymperii* plasters its eggs on bark above its web and a smaller, rarer, yellow-brown comb-footed mountaineer, *Theridian bellicosum*, dwells among the stones up Coniston's Old Man. *Amaurobius atropus* and *Monocephalus castaneipes*, not specially mountainous species, burrow under stones up to the summits of Helvellyn and Scafell, and the common wolf-spider *Pirata piraticus*, with its conspicuous white egg-sac, hunts from under herbage at 2,600ft on Saddleback.

Plants

The first alpine plants to bloom are the purple saxifrages, from February to Easter—climbers who fail to count petals mistake them for aubretia. They may be found in numerous places, including Helvellyn's central crags. It is perhaps the aim of finding one's first purple saxifrage in its natural haunts before seeing plants of it at the Alpine Garden Society's shows at Harrogate and Southport that brings the mountains back to life after their winter silence. Many gardeners grow the alpines they buy much better after seeing their natural habitat—a hanging position that is quickly drained and is shaded from strong sunlight.

For the best floral display one must seek the volcanic ash and basic rocks, guided by indicator plants such as fleshy roseroot and green spleenwort fern, or even by litmus paper, working upstream to find the sweeter soil. The arctic-alpine treasures rooting in seemingly bare rock crevices on the shaded faces of Helvellyn, Wastwater Screes, Pillar and Fairfield rival the rich flora of the limestone fells, but mostly have a shorter flowering season in early summer. Eskdale granite and acid Bowfell (except Hell Ghyll above Stool End farm in Langdale), Buttermere and Ennerdale syenite, Skiddaw slate, Blencathra, Grassmoor, Great Gable, Robinson and Hinscarth are far less productive than the basic rocks, mostly on the shaded north or east faces of the mountains. The summit of Helvellyn is featureless.

One's first view of Lakeland when approaching from the south is of the peaks of Furness ranging westwards to Black Combe. The Old Man of Coniston (the name a corruption of Allt Main, the chief mountain) has had much of the vegetation tramped off its Dow Crag by the cleated boots of an almost endless procession of summer climbers from Church Beck. At Church Beck, the last haunt of royal fern, where butterworts flower freely, one meets the junipers and the sundews, above the youth hostel. Starry saxifrage may be seen among stagshorns, fir and little clubmosses. One may go on through the saddle, finding more flowers near Low Water and the track above the quarry, or travel from the stream up Walna Scar Road and turn left along the track skirting the foot of Little Arrow Moor, an extensive prehistoric settlement, coming to a gently sloping shelf between gradually steepening slopes north to Goatswater.

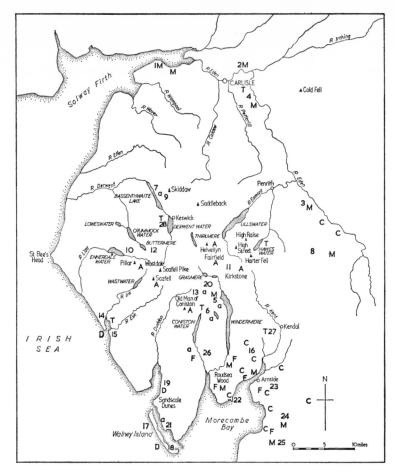

Fig 4   Plant distribution

1. Glasson Moss	19. Roanhead Dunes
2. Scaleby Moss	20. Elterwater
3. Cliburn Moss	21. Cavendish Dock, Barrow
4. Carleton and Cumwhitton Mosses	22. Humphrey Head
5. Blelham Tarn and Bog	23. Arnside Knott
6. Esthwaite North Fen	24. Silverdale Quarry
7. Bassenthwaite	25. Hale Moss
8. Orton Scar	26. Rusland Valley
9. Ivy Crag Wood, Under Skiddaw	27. Brightsea Wood
10. Ennerdale Liza Valley	28. Birkrigg and Keskadale Oaks
11. Red Screes	
12. Honister Pass	
13. Tilberthwaite Gill	A. Alpines
14. Drigg Dunes	a. Aquatics
15. Eskmeals Dunes	C. Calcicoles
16. Whitbarrow and Scout Scar	D. Dunes
17. Biggar Bank	F. Ferns
18. South Walney Dunes	M. Mossland and bog
	T. Trees (deciduous and exotic)

Here I have looked in vain for the white mountain orchid, but spotted heath orchid is common.

Dwarf willow is an arctic survival on the ridge of Dow Crag, 2,555ft, which is too acid for much mountain flora. Hoary whitlow grass and roseroot choose calcareous crags at 1,800–2,000ft; red alpine catchfly may linger, but yellow mountain saxifrage is extinct. Much of Dow Crag's flora is poor, though both filmy ferns survive, and pink bird's-eye primrose grows sparingly. The blue meadow-grass *glauca* grows at 1,760ft, and alpine scurvy grass shares wet fissures with the moss *Philmotis fontana*. Creeping New Zealand willowherb *nerterioides* has colonised the streams, and plenty of parsley fern and the moss *Rhaconitrium lanuginosum* mark the screes. Lichens on the slate include *Gyrophora cylindrica*, *Rhizocarpon geographicum* and *Lecanora atra*. Even wood crowfoot grows high among the roseroot, with woodsorrel and wood sage.

Bird's-eye primrose also grows on calcareous rock near Tilberthwaite Gill, and at the boggy east end of Ennerdale Lake. Its other locations include the calcareous marl at the Hawes Water end of Silverdale's Red Bridge lane, at Wansfell near Ambleside, and the moor at Sunbiggin Tarn.

With an abundance of green volcanic ash and breccia, Kirkstone Pass has starry, mossy and yellow mountain saxifrages by the wayside to Brotherswater, alpine scurvy grass near its 1,300ft summit, mountain cranesbill on its cliff-face, and fir clubmoss and New Zealand willowherb by Caistor Beck. The Red Screes beyond should not be confused with a similarly named plant-area on Helvellyn. Scafell, climbed from Seatoller via Seathwaite, Taylor Ghyll and Sty Head Tarn, dominates the central mountains, though its height of 3,210ft is only one-fifth that of Mont Blanc. It is less rich in flowers than Helvellyn's Nethermost Cove and other areas, but it has alpine lady's mantle, and in the ghylls of the great ravines in its flanks are stone bramble, and Wilson's filmy fern. Purple saxifrage colours its crags, moss campion in pink-studded close cushions is plentiful, but mountain dryas almost extinct. Lakeland's advantage over Switzerland where mountain flowers are concerned is that alpines grow lowest in the northernmost parts of their range, and you must climb about 4,000ft to see moss campion in the Swiss Alps, 2,400ft to see yellow mountain saxifrage and 3,600ft for alpine lady's mantle.

Helvellyn's flowers are not to be seen along its well-trodden 3,118ft summit but in its craggy northern and eastern (Westmorland) coves and on its broken slopes. Alpine saxifrage, alpine mouse-eared chickweed (above Red Tarn), downy and dwarf willows, alpine catstail, meadow grass, *Poa balfouri*, black sedge, the alpine eyebright *frigida*, the mountain variety of thyme-leaved speedwell, and mountain bladder and holly ferns are to be found. *Poa glauca* grows to 2,800ft, where occasionally alpine pennycress is found. Purple saxifrage is probably at its best among the cliffs, which it shares with whitlow grass, roseroot, thrift, vernal sandwort, kidney vetch, serrated wintergreen, moss campion, mountain everlasting and globe flowers. Alpine meadow rue, mistaken by climbers for maidenhair fern, and moss campion grow in coves under Dolywaggon Pike at 2,810ft, and on the calcareous ledges of Catchedicum and Brown Cove. Alpine willowherb appears at 1,800ft by Raise Beck. Above Red Tarn the mountain bladder fern is now rare, but there are alpine hawkweeds *holosericeum* and *subgracilentipes*, as well as alpine *Saussurea* and creeping forget-me-not.

At 2,500–3,000ft the Red Screes harbour mossy and starry saxifrages, water avens, roseroot, thrift, mountain sorrel, alpine *Saussurea*, vernal sandwort and black sedge. Three-flowered rush grows at 2,000ft at Catchedicum on the north side of Red Tarn. The experienced alpine plant-hunter is not surprised to find humble woodsorrel at 2,750ft, even in its mauve form, with other lowlanders like water starwort by Red Tarn, and wood anemones on the crags. But shrubby cinquefoil may be extinct here.

Fairfield's 2,863ft, where moss campion blooms in June, looks best from Deepdale in the rocky north, but is easiest to approach from the grassy south, or the Travellers' Rest at Grasmere and Grizedale Tarn, or from Ambleside via Low Pike, High Pike and Hart Crag. Here again is sea campion, with catsfoot at 1,700ft, alpine *Saussurea*, and whitlow grass. Alpine cinquefoil is abundant on its crags, as are kidney vetch, northern bedstraw and the usual alpines. (Should you be caught in mist, beware of the precipices on the Deepdale side—look for Grizedale Tarn and follow its safe track back to Patterdale. The distress signal anywhere is six long whistle-blasts or torch-flashes repeated after one minute.)

A walk across the moors by Watendlath or Blea Tarn to the brink of the fell, with the peakless mass of Helvellyn above, affords a better view of Thirlmere than does the road below. Pillar, the big hump of black rock, blocks the head of Mosedale at 2,927ft. Upper Ennerdale at the head of the Buttermere valley has a few good northern-plant crags, with roseroot, alpine *Saussurea*, mountain sorrel, mossy, starry and the yellow mountain saxifrages, goldenrod, alpine and lesser meadow rues, and alpine campion among the usual great woodrush, wild thyme and dog violets. Shrubby cinquefoil, dwarf willow and jointed rush also bloom, as does cat's ear on Watendlath Fell.

The slopes of St Sunday Crag, 2,756ft above Patterdale and Grizedale display lady's mantle (whose seeds nibbling sheep distribute in their droppings), cowberry, dwarf willow, oblong Woodsia, mossy and the yellow mountain saxifrages, and grass-of-parnassus. The latter's white cups may also be found at Watendlath, and catsfoot in a boulder crevice by the beck. Parts of the Borrowdale cliffs beyond Seatoller are enriched with calcium and, in consequence, alpine lady's mantle grows at 2,000ft near the summit, on the volcanic fells, and also with serrated wintergreen in the dry crevices of gullies from 1,000 to 1,700ft (as well as in Mardale's Vale of Legburthwaite). Borrowdale also accommodates alpine clubmoss, melancholy thistle, bog orchid, long-leaved sundew and carnivorous lesser bladderwort at their respective levels. Bogbean grows as high as Glaramara, reached from Seatoller and Seathwaite over Allen Crags at the head of Borrowdale, and yellow mountain saxifrage at 1,200ft on damp ground on Armboth Fell, and in Yewdale.

Lakeland has many Grisedales, old haunts of the wolf, and starry saxifrage specks the damp bilberry ground about the 2,593ft summit of Grisedale Pike from Braithwaite near Keswick. Beyond this rises Grasmoor, with bearberry among the heather and juniper of its rocky western slope, and sea campion with alpine lady's mantle in its screes.

Between Grasmoor and Grisedale Pike and rising above the Whinlatter Pass, is Hobcarton Pike, the first-known English site for alpine campion (the red alpine catchfly), which flowers among cowberry on the steep eastern side of two gullies marked by quartz veins in their slate. The rest of its flora is less interesting.

Honister Crag has sea plantain, which grows also on sandy banks up Ennerdale, on its barren ledges, as well as mountain everlasting or catsfoot, starry and mossy saxifrages, mountain sorrel, alpine lady's mantle and purple mountain pansy above the Pass, and yellow mountain saxifrage on the quarry scree below. Mountain pansy appears also on Robinson Crag above Buttermere.

To the north, Skiddaw ('Little Man') is 3,058ft of mainly dry acid slopes, but it has alpine campion in sunny gullies at 2,000–2,300ft, forked spleenwort fern at the base of the slates (as at Llanrwst in North Wales), and cloudberry, also found on Matterdale Common. Barrenwort is found here, and also grows on Carrock and Wasdale Screes, and a dwarf 2in goldenrod grows on the flat slate summit. Nearly fifty ravens occupied this area in the winter of 1971.

To the west, Wastwater or Wasdale Screes form a splendid chaos of frost-torn rocks, running for nearly 2 miles on the north-west front of Whin Rigg (on the western slopes of Illgill Head) and poised above the lake. These rocks are among the few remaining sites of shrubby cinquefoil, formerly widely distributed in Lakeland at places like Pillar and up the Red Screes gully. Yellow and purple mountain saxifrages, barrenwort, northern rock cress seen in shining white clumps long after the earlier alpines are over, moonwort, roseroot, grass-of-parnassus, water avens and others grow mainly in gullies of calcareous outcrops in the hard acid volcanic rock at 1,300–1,500ft, along with royal fern, columbine, shepherd's cress and dropwort. Alpine meadow rue is also found in the heights above the River Liza, east of Ennerdale Lake.

To the east, the north-east face of High Street has pyramidal bugle on a ledge between 1,000ft and 2,500ft, and black sedge and moss campion at 2,500ft. Alpine meadow rue and holly fern grow on Blea Tarn crags, with hoary whitlow grass and cloud-berry among the cotton-grass at 2,000ft. Three-flowered rush grows at 1,900ft on Caudde Moor, with bog whortleberries, which, of course, grow much lower nearer Carlisle. Bird's-eye primrose graces some of the dales, marsh violets the soft slope of Lady's Seat and wild thyme the harder rocks. Chickweed willowherb and globe flower may be seen on Shap Fell; holly fern on Rough Crag, Harter Fell and Nan Bield Pass; her-maphrodite crowberry is found 1,200ft up Riggindale Screes, one of its several locations; and cloudberry on Leck Fell above Kirkby Lonsdale.

Cross Fell, whose plateau is the meeting-place of the cold wet helm-wind (named from the parallel Helm Bar of cloud resting along the range) from the east and the warm west wind from the sea, has ridges of parsley fern (less common as one approaches the Pennines and leaves the red sandstone ridge of Penrith), cloudberries, alpine willowherb and the short-leaved northern water forget-me-not *brevifolia*, which also grows at 2,000ft on the Kentdale side of Howter Fell, on Cross Fell and near Shap. Cold Fell at the northern end of the Pennines is another cloudberry site.

Spring gentian and brilliant blue alpine forget-me-nots sparkle high on the limestone eastern sides of Mickle Fell and Little Fell, above Hilton on the Westmorland–Durham border, an area best approached from Teesdale. Spring gentian was found at Alston Moor in 1958, an outlier of the Pennine limestone flora, as was a now-extinct site of lady's slipper near Keswick. Mickle Fell also has its moonwort fern, which often grows high on mountain ledges, plus chickweed willowherb, England's only spathulate fleawort, hoary whitlow grass, and alpine forget-me-not on its high limestone west end above Hilton, Westmorland. Chickweed willowherb grows also on the Kentmere Fells as well as at Buttermere and Whinlatter. Tiny least willow and three-flowered rush grow on Kentmere Fells.

Dove Crag, a scramble between Hart Crag and Fairfield, has alpine meadow rue, alpine lady's mantle and sea campion. At 2,000ft on calcareous rock here and at Hartsop grow alpine pennycress and alpine mouse-eared chickweed, and hermaphrodite crowberry inhabits screes at 1,800ft, as does the dwarf willow. Globe flower and spignel-meum (bald-money) grow west of the Shap road. The field botanist does not spend his time hunting for rare plants, though it is exciting to see one for the first time. His main purpose is to study the flora, perhaps to rummage round the plants of each mountain at least once. Bowfell is not among the places he *must* visit, but viviparous alpine bistort grows there at over 1,800ft, and there is also interrupted clubmoss, which grows too in Rossett Ghyll and up Great Langdale on the grassy slopes among damp rocks.

The mountains hold a great variety of ferns. Apart from the Durham border of Upper Teesdale where it has not been seen in recent years, the only English haunts of oblong Woodsia (*ilvensis*) are St Sunday Crag and near Crosby Ravensworth church.

Not all the plants one encounters are favourites with rock gardeners. The scaly clubmosses certainly are not. Relics of the pre-glacial flora that reached their zenith in Carboniferous times, they are much commoner than in southern England, and include alpine clubmoss near the 1,800ft summit of Mainden Moor, Borrowdale, as well as the more localised interrupted clubmoss mentioned above. Fir clubmoss is common in the higher turf, as in Kirkstone Pass. Then there is stone bramble in Kirk Fell and Scafell ghylls, oak fern on the lower slopes of Wansfell Pike, and least rush and dwarf goldenrod on one of the summits of Skiddaw slate. Roseroot is sought as an indicator of basic rock, without waiting for it to bear its yellow flowers.

Page 71 (*above*) The reedy jingle of the cock yellowhammer's song marks the fellsides from spring to autumn. Distinguished as much by its russet rump as its yellow head, it now joins chaffinches to feed on tourists' scraps at car-parks; (*below*) a woodcock using its stick-like beak to feed on earthworms

Page 72 (*above*) The male dotterel, a migratory bird-of-passage, visiting former nesting haunts on the eastern mountains; (*below*) the return of the nesting lapwing to the fells is a sign of spring. Frosts and snowstorms drive flocks into the western estuaries or to milder Ireland

It grows at 2,200ft on Esk Hause Pass and on Helvellyn Crags, on Coniston heights, above the ridge east of Ennerdale, on the Pillar of Ennerdale, and on Wasdale Screes.

Lichens and Mosses

The lichenologist will find a score of his species around Scafell Pike cairn, along with half a dozen mosses Lakeland is not noted for many alpine lichen species, though Langdale is the only British haunt of *Umbilicaria crustulosa*. There is doubt whether true reindeer moss, the lichen *Cladonia rangiferina*, grows in Lakeland, though it appears at 2,000ft on Greygarth Fell in north Lancashire, as well as on Ward's Stone and Wolfhole Crag.

The narrow wet limestone gorges of Aisgill and Hell Gill on the Yorkshire border of Westmorland's Upper Eden Valley are rich in mosses. Vast sheets of *Orthothecium rufescens* drape the sandstone rocks above the old railway viaduct, as well as the dripping wet ravine of Aisgill above the B6259, at the head of Mallerstang Common and below Wild Boar Fell. It shares the gorge with masses of common *Crotoneuron commutatum* and such uncommon mosses as the alpine flat fork-moss *Fissidens osmundoides*, the beardless moss *Gymnostomum aeruginosum*, the thyme thread-moss *Mnium longisostrum*, the apple-mosses *Bartramia halleriana* and *B. pomiformis*, and *Diphyscium foliosum*, *Ditrichium flexicaule*, *Blindia acuta*, and others. That typical limestone indicator *Neckera crispa* luxuriates with curly leaved screw-moss, *Tortula tortuosa*, on the limestone cliffs on both sides of the B6259. Golden green *Ctenidium milluscum* and the thyme thread-moss *Mnium undulatum* tolerate the sandstone as well. The hair-moss *Polytrichum urnigerum* grows in Aisgill quarry, and the rare little *Seligeria pusilla* is common on the fellside above the gorge.

Quarries, especially limestone, have as much botanical as geological interest. The Crown Quarry at Stainton, near Dalton in Furness, and Silverdale Quarry above Storrs Moss are examples. Although the common *Sphagna* bog mosses are most numerous

E

on low fells and raised bogs or 'Mosses', some species ascend very high—*Sphagnum obesum* at 2,000ft in Eskdale—while others, such as the brightly coloured variety of *S. auriculatum* under the trees beside Rydal Water, are lowlanders.

CHAPTER FIVE

Forests

A FOREST DOES not have to be densely wooded, with tall pines thrown over the hills like great rugs. Martindale deer forest has only a few little spinneys of bedraggled wind-torn trees affording shelter from neither bitter helm-winds nor stinging hailstones. The last of England's uncultivated deer 'forests' in the Scottish sporting style, it illustrates the old Mardalian saying: 'From Rampsgill Ridge is but a cockstride to a Martindale stag'.

Grizedale Deer Forest, which has covered open fellside above Hawkshead with woodland in our time, typifies the modern plantation, and has become a natural haunt of red deer. Such dark woods, where one steps into cathedral-like tranquillity, have increased roe, buzzard and blackcock populations and may be the salvation of red squirrel and pine marten. Green palaces of larch in spring lure invading crossbills to stay and nest, from Ambleside to Skelwith Bridge. Rides of coppiced sessile oak and birch redden Furness and the south Cumbrian hills in the autumn. The southern wood-ant *rufa* burrows beneath the limestone yews of Arnside Park, at Eggerslack and the conifer woods at Grange, and heaps its remarkable pine-needle nests there as well as north to Windermere, Skiddaw Forest above Bassenthwaite, and round Appleby and Caldbeck. The northern wood-ant *lugubris* lives in Dunnerdale and the Ashness woods above Derwentwater, though we meet it also in North Wales, and the shining black ant *fuliginosa* ranges to Arnside, Grange and Yewdale.

Roudsea Wood by the Leven comprises 287 acres of Britain's most varied woodland on two parallel ridges. One ridge is limestone, where yew, ash and oak shelter lilies-of-the-valley and fly orchids, and brimstone butterflies, hosts of moths, many roe and occasionally fallow and red deer congregate. The other ridge supports old coppiced oak and boggy tarns with yellow sedge, and changes from wood to saltmarsh seawards, and wood to Holker Moss peat inland. Deerdike and Fish House mosslands are important here.

Great trees thrive in the rain, and Thirlmere has 90in of rain per annum, three times the lowland figure. One of my pleasures when staying at Monk Coniston Hall is to stroll among its 13 acres of specimen trees, of which a dozen conifers have gained a place on the Forestry Commission records. Britain has no taller Himalayan silver fir *Abies pindrow* than that standing 90ft high and 9ft 1in round on the Hall's lawn. England's tallest western hemlock *Isuga heterophyla* here stands 127ft high, and the blue tree below it is the rare mountain hemlock *Isuga mertensiana*, 50ft high in the early 1960s.

Some rocky land will not grow worthwhile hardwoods, though the Windermere basin is an amenity zone for them, and badger and roe favour Tower Wood. The forest areas mostly fringe the central mountains, stretching chiefly from Ennerdale to Windermere and Floriston (increasing the chaffinch's habitat). Fell-walkers criticise the afforestation that has created the northern Border Forest Park (with Kershope Forest, and Sapeadam Waste), Hardknott National Forest Park, and the woods of Thornthwaite, Ennerdale, etc, complaining of attempts to create unnatural replicas of the Black Forest when it would have been better to have left the wild irregular native woodland alone. Yet the beautiful autumn tints admired on oak, ash, sycamore, alder, hazel, willow, and rowan from High Furness to Grange and Barrow are the reward of equally artificial coppicing for bobbin-mills, casks and charcoal until about 1927. Conifers climb far up Wasdale and towards Great Gable, over Honister Pass and into Lorton Vale.

Naddle Low Forest near Hawes Water is probably the only surviving primitive forest of ash, oak and mountain birch on slate in a region of high rainfall, and possesses the rarer mosses like the ostrich-plume *Ptilium* and *Hylocomium umbratum*. Lindale near Cartmel and Lindal near Ulverston take their names from the lime tree, a doubtful native, and Musgrave in Westmorland means the mouse-wood. Juniper is common from the slopes of Coniston Old Man to Yewdale, and birch regenerates freely on acid soils, an attraction to redpolls. Lower Borrowdale is enhanced by many silver birches.

The Forestry Commission, under the Northwest Conservancy at Chester, made its finest Lakeland forest at Thornthwaite—5,400 acres of spruce, larch, pine and Douglas fir stretching round Bassenthwaite, over the Whinlatter Pass and far up the foothills of Skiddaw. Here the diminishing rattle of the nightjar and comb-rasping calls of the corncrake are heard, and badgers may be seen.

Ivy Crag Wood at Under Skiddaw (Cumberland) is the northernmost location for spurge laurel, and autumn lady's tresses and squinancy wort grow in parts of old Lancashire which are north of Westmorland. The more glamorous *Daphne mezereum* grows in woods near Carlisle and Penrith, on Whitbarrow Scar, among oak and ash scrub at Silverdale and with *laureola* near Kendal.

The Lakes have interesting deciduous woods like Ullock birch-moss, Ashness oak wood at Derwentwater, Burtness and Horseclose oak woods at Buttermere, Greengate old oak wood at Wasdale, Holme and Watering oak woods at Loweswater, Lanthwaite oak wood, Scale Wood (Crummock), and Glencoyne (Ullswater). Near Kendal are Brightseer and Cunswick oak-ash woods, with lesser butterfly orchids, and others include Johnny's Wood in Borrowdale and Gelt Woods in the northeast near the A69.

Other Cumberland forests include Ennerdale, where spruce woods rise from the lake at Bowness Point, Miterdale and Dunnerdale. Roe had become established in Gilberthwaite

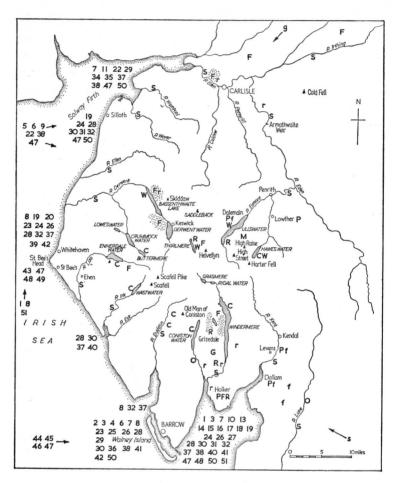

Fig 5   Mammal and fish habitats

KEYS TO MAP OPPOSITE

1. Bass
2. Sea Bream
3. Short-spined Sea Scorpion
4. Yellow Gurnard
5. Armed Bullhead (Pogge)
6. Angler
7. Lesser Weever
8. Mackerel
9. Horse Mackerel (Scad)
10. Gobies
11. Dragonet
12. Blenny
13. Shanney
14. Butterfish
15. Sand Smelt
16. Three-Spined Stickleback
17. Fifteen-Spined Stickleback
18. Grey Mullet
19. Cod, Codling
20. Haddock
21. Pout (Bib)
22. Poor Cod
23. Coalfish
24. Whiting
25. Pollack
26. Rocklings
27. Sand Eel
28. Plaice
29. Lemon Sole
30. Dab
31. Flounder (Fluke)
32. Sole
33. Solenette

34. Turbot
35. Brill
36. Long-nosed Pipefish
37. Sea Trout
38. Sparling (smelt)
39. Herring
40. Sprat
41. Twaite Shad
42. Freshwater Eel
43. Conger
44. Blue Shark
45. Porbeagle
46. Basking Shark
47. Lesser Spotted Dogfish
48. Monk
49. Skate
50. Thornback Ray
51. Tope

C. Char
F. Forests
f. Fallow Deer
g. Feral Goats
G. Greythwaite (deer)
M. Martindale Deer Forest
O. Otter
P. Deer Park
R. Red Deer
r. Roe Deer
S. Salmon
s. Sika Deer
W. Whitefish (Coregonus)

Forest in Ennerdale by 1950 and at Lowther Forest near Egremont (not to be confused with Lowther Castle). The pine marten was seen in Halle Woods near Egremont and another 5 miles over the fells in the Calder Valley. The nightjar and the sparrowhawk linger here as nesters and up to five pairs of buzzards breed. There are two long-standing peregrine eyries and three ravenages (Floutern Crags), and there was once a heronry near the lake.

The big wood near Floriston railway signal-box, north of Carlisle, has roe deer, which I found are not rare, but shy and secretive, to be watched at dusk or dawn. The sunny southern end of the wood shelters them from the helm-wind. The rides or paths across this fir wood beside the A47 are rough with ling, golden-brown tufts of wood rush and spearlike bog rushes; and the deep peaty dykes beside them are bordered with northern hard fern. The last great wood in England, its tall black pines are interspersed with pure stands of larch, and with the graceful acid-loving birch. At dusk a family of roe, buck and doe and one or two fawns, no more, used to leave the wood to find more succulent feeding up the valley of the Esk in the night. Their remarkable leaping powers made it almost impossible to fence them into a wood or out of a garden, and they had no fear of traffic along the busy road to Gretna. A wood without deer is like a house without furniture, or a garden without flowers.

Red deer inhabit Thirlmere's 2,000 acre forest, but, at least recently, there have been no roe this side of Helvellyn. A few red squirrels may be found among Thirlmere's Douglas fir and Norway spruce, Corsican pine, western hemlock, European and reddish-tinged Japanese larch. One used to admire its few stags or Sandy, the great Clydesdale horse, dragging felled trees down its slopes. Its thirty to forty deer usually range the tops of the Armboth fells, west of the lake. Foresters and deer do not get on well together, and some culling is necessary, for even the beeches up the eastern side of the lake have had their bark chewed. Two nature trails run through the forest—the Swirls and Launchy Ghyll. Over 120 nest-boxes attract pied flycatchers and titmice, and ravens and buzzards nest in the higher parts. Like most Lakeland forests, it is the home of badgers as well as of foxes. Before the war, Manchester planted larches up its slopes of Helvellyn.

The rocky outcrop on Claife Heights commands views down the long length of Lake Windermere and up to the heights of Coniston and Bowfell, where the Pikes of Langdale stab the sky. The way from Ferry House on the north-west shore of the lake to Belle Grange takes one past yellow balsam thriving in the rain. There is a two-way badger gate in the fence before one enters the forest and climbs the hill pass through Well Head plantation. Red and roe deer soon reveal themselves by their tracks and by the barked and top-nibbled young larches. Twenty reds and some forty roe live here, and Lakeland's post-World War II record stag of 30 stones was shot on Claife Heights.

The Forestry Commission has a treetop ('high-seat') deer-observation platform in the oak wood below Scale Head and another over the hill. In this wood, darkened by fir and furze, live badger and woodcock, green and pied woodpeckers; tree-creepers hitch their way up the trunks and buzzards circle overhead. Bullfinches are also to be seen, and the endless songs from goldcrest and cole tit are audible until the bridle-path finally leads one to Belle Grange and human contact.

In Furness are the forests of Lindale, Dalton and, most important, the 7,440 acres or $11\frac{3}{4}$sq miles of Grizedale, which includes a camp-site beside the Satterthwaite–Hawkshead road, a deer museum, a 1 mile forest trail, the Ridding Wood Nature Trail and an observation tower for deer-watchers. Pied fly-catchers use the nest-boxes along the oak-fringed eastern forest road, where 40 aggressive long-tailed Reeves pheasants have been naturalised, as have 52 Scottish capercaillie from Moray elsewhere in the forest. But these tend to wander off, as far as Monk Coniston. On one expedition we rose at 3 am and crossed the forest to creep behind a stone wall high up the open fell between Coniston Water and Esthwaite to see a blackcocks' lek, a trysting-ground, where up to six of these aggressive black grouse would put on a display—unless the wind was too strong. As this was in earlier years, when our cars were permitted in the forest, we crawled along until, only 10yd ahead, we could see in the dim beam of the headlight on the forest road high above Brantwood a blackcock's plumage glisten with purple as it spread its lyre-shaped tail, and the scarlet skin above its eyes glow like fire as it scratched for grit. Below Hawkshead Hill that time we came upon a red stag in velvet, the knobs of his new antlers showing plainly as he stood barely 20yd away in the thin morning mist. Yet in the forest by day, when deer and blackcock lie up, there is little evidence of earlier happenings.

A stag of 26 stones was shot here in 1961, and his weight compares favourably with the 16 stone of the Scottish 'Monarch of the Glen'. Thick dark antlers distinguish Grizedale from Martindale stags, which have thin grey ones. Some 200 roe share the forest with badgers, red squirrels and numerous foxes. Its 200 red deer show an increasing population, whereas the roe—and the blackcock—are static. Pine martens have twice been seen, and a little muntjac deer, which had escaped from captivity, was seen near the southern border. The head forester told me of his liberation of eight polecats, which had died out in Lakeland. Mallard, teal and introduced greylags breed on the forest tarn, where Carolina wood duck may be added; and half a dozen buzzards breed also. Like cole tits, they are much commoner in southern than in northern Lakeland.

In 1937 the formerly poor grazing of Grizedale began to be turned into rich forest, reaching 1,200ft above sea level, with 70in of rain a year. In clearings we may see its butterflies—speckled wood and pearl-bordered fritillary, orange-tip in spring and small tortoiseshell in winter. By its pools may be dragonflies—blue demoiselle, four-spotted *Libellula* and black or Scottish *Sympetrum*. Raven and redstart inhabit the wood, with green and great spotted woodpeckers, nightjar and woodcock; and Britain's most northerly golden oriole nest was found here in 1958–9.

Woodcock are widespread in Lakeland, particularly in Tarn

Hows Wood, where ten or twelve pairs have nested. They are also found beside the road at Rydal and over the mossy shades of Lingholme, where herons used to nest beside Derwentwater above Portinscale. Here also was a gabble of garden warblers and blackcaps, and pied flycatchers occupied a lakeside tree. A white woodcock was shot on Windermere's south shore in 1923, and another albino in Cumberland in 1932.

From Witherslack, near Grange, northwards, about 100 pairs of roe and more than 100 red deer dwell in other woods among the fells. Finsthwaite is a good base for exploring this roe country, tucked away among wooded knolls and heather-clad fells between south Windermere and Coniston. Roe spend the day ligging in the dim larch woods, and creep out at dusk. They are best seen at daybreak, though a sudden bark or stamp of foot may reveal the white stern of a roe bobbing away in the steep hill-wood between Newby Bridge and Finsthwaite Tower. In May one may find a newly dropped fawn in the same bed of bracken year after year—Old Hag Wood where the road curls round the woods and hills to Rusland is such a spot. Other roe signs are the circles and figure-of-eight rings made by the bucks' rutting chase of the does round some hillock beneath the oak trees. Once these sessile oak woods were dotted with charcoal-kilns, which fired the earliest iron industry of Furness. Later they were coppiced for the local bobbin industry, until the Forestry Commission planted acres of pitprop-larches, and shot the roe they harboured because of the damage they caused.

The wind is one's first consideration in deer-watching. Let us pass through the woods of Finsthwaite Heights, then across the rocky moors, where grayling butterflies flicker, and over mile after mile of purple and mauve heath and heather with the north-west wind in one's face. Ahead lies a scramble of peaks from the Old Man by Fairfield to the deer tracks on Cartmel Fell. No red grouse, woodcock or badger are here, but the trees are noisy with jays and green woodpeckers and the cat-cry of the buzzard drifts down from the sky. Bogs fragrant with sweet gale occasionally reveal grass-of-parnassus. At night the fierce spider *Drassodes lapidosus* prowls from under stones and dry clumps of grass in Thornthwaite and other forests, while black-spotted yellow *Ciniflo fenestralis* hides in bark and *Zygiella atrica* commonly spins a web with a slice out of it.

The ling powders one's boots grey with pollen until one reaches the red stag's country at Greythwaite, an estate of 7,000 acres running to Far Sawry, which protects its red deer from shooting. Stags here rarely grow more than 12 points, but, improved by Warnham Court blood, their heads have grown less ugly than those of the original Martindale stock. Their favourite spots are Dale Park Fell, Bishop's Wood and even the drive near the hall. Roe are present also, and once a party of seven came to the field below the keeper's house.

The stag at eve can drink his fill at several moorland trout-tarns—Bore Tree, with its wild duck, reached through thickets of juniper and dwarf furze above Yew Barrow; Big Dam, which one comes upon suddenly through the tapering larches on Finsthwaite Heights; and, at Greythwaite, the top tarn at Green Hows, where a few blackcock dwell. Three pairs of buzzards bred on Greythwaite estate, and one morning thirty-seven red deer were seen on the hill of Cran Brow Wood, above Eel House, and a dozen above Esthwaite Hall Farm at Elwood Planting. One often sees the Greythwaite red deer from the road.

Buzzards nested for at least ten years in the Lag Wood above Coniston, and others at Rydal, Skelwith Bridge and, with sparrowhawks and long-eared owls, in Blakeholme Plantation, Newby Bridge.

Crossbills in the big invasion in the 1950s bred in the larches of Guards Wood. In summer, when the breast-high bracken is greenest, the roe are as red as foxes, but in winter they hide themselves in coats of hodden grey. Shy and powerless after shedding their short stabbing antlers, they normally freeze into immobility for protection. Against white snow, however, they are restlessly aware of their lack of camouflage. Slots or foot-prints crisscross the Finsthwaite woods, where they paw through snow for sustenance, even toadstools, and their tracks over white fields reveal deer-paths trodden out years ago. Having traversed the Greythwaite woods to Grubbins Point, with snow-streaked Gummer's How gazing over the frozen face of Winder-mere, except for a patch of open water harbouring its goldeneye, tufted duck and goosanders, one can turn up the lakeside through Cunsey Woods, where roe bound away like gazelles. Their presence is also shown by droppings or fewmets, and trees barked by older bucks irritated by the velvet on their new antlers. After dark one sees them from the roadside outlined in the adjoining woods.

The woods vary from coniferous country ripe for autumn fungus-forays around Tarn Hows and Thirlmere, yet with long dark stretches, inhabited by occasional roving flocks of titmice, which find few natural nest-holes in summer unless bird-boxes are provided, to lighter deciduous woods like Roudsea in Furness, and Glencoyne, where pied flycatchers nest beyond Patterdale and Wilson's filmy fern and the mud sedge grow, and the alien *Saxifraga cymbalaria* has established itself beside the stream. Grizedale conifer forest is the best for vertebrate fauna, and Roudsea Wood, of oak and ash, for flora and Lepidoptera. The latter wood is rich in fly orchids and rock-rose, and has one of the only two British sites (a wet valley in the limestone) of the yellow sedge *flava*. It has also at least seventeen species of fern, including royal fern and adder's tongue. Herb paris, marsh andromeda, ploughman's spikenard and lilies-of-the-valley are others of its flora. It is also rich in roe.

Squirrels, wood-carder bees and fritillary and purple hair-streak butterflies prosper in Eggerslack Wood above Grange, where the Forestry Commission underplanted limestone beech, oak, sycamore and ash with tsuga and thuya to take out as thinnings when the hardwoods were middle-aged, and whence the fire of autumn burns up the Winster Valley into the heart of Lakeland.

Scattered pine and larch extend the woods by driving their roots among exposed bare rocks on the upper limits and building up soil formerly eroded away by sheep-grazing. This has happened at Hampsfell (Hampsfield Fell) and Dalton (towards Kirkby Lonsdale crags). The naturalist sees the dense plantation of alien conifers and the more natural deciduous wood as shelter and food for Lakeland wildlife. He sees the change the Forestry Commission and Manchester Corporation water department have brought to former sheep-walks and open heathland unsentimentally, feeling that many of the criticisms made of the commission's work a generation ago are no longer valid after what has happened at Grizedale, and in reverse at Lowther. Closely planted conifer woods attract most birds in their first ten to twenty years, then most birds are shaded out unless they have an amenity fringe of oak like Grizedale.

Most Lakeland red squirrels are of purer native stock than the crossbreds that have appeared with the liberation of Continental pets in the Yorkshire dales and south-west Lancashire pines. Approachable in the Boot area of Eskdale, they may be seen also at Glencoyne, Latrigg (Keswick), Holker, Grasmere, Storrs, Windermere, Silverdale's Hawes Water, Greystoke Castle, Penrith (1970), and other woods. They are now recovering from a decline that occurred about 1950. The Carolina grey squirrel, which appeared at Ambleside in 1961 and previously at Wansfell and the Lowther estate, is a deciduous woodlander and is unlikely to colonise the pine forests. Early in World War II one was shot near Carnforth, to the south.

The early stages of conifer plantation encourage the short-tailed field voles and bank voles, which bring their predators, the breeding short-eared owls and buzzards. Voles are subject to albinism, and Carlisle Museum also has specimens of white hedgehog and the long-tailed wood mouse, which, in contradiction to its name *sylvestris* and its haunts, is misnamed field-mouse. Despite an unacceptable claim from a location near Carnforth in 1924, the wild wood-cat has been long extinct; but enormous depredation upon birdlife in Lakeland is now caused by the ever-increasing population of feral domestic cats. I saw one in Grizedale Forest in 1972. Such a cat, 3ft long, had been living wild for months according to newspaper headlines when sheep farmers shot it at Selside, Westmorland, one night in May 1935, after beagles, otterhounds and foxhounds had failed to track it down. It was accused, with some exaggeration, of killing lambs, a charge more recently laid against the golden eagles around High Street and against foxes. A dog fox weighing 22lb, killed in the hills near Barrow in April 1956, had its mask set up by a Clitheroe taxidermist. White foxes are rare, but a white vixen killed by Ullswater Hounds in 1964 left a white cub, and a white fox was killed by Coniston Hounds on Hawkshead Moor in 1947.

As we have said, the extension of forests and the control of gin-traps, together with the decline of gamekeeping, has aided the pine marten's recovery, from Ennerdale to Kentmere Dalehead, Loweswater, Troutbeck, Ullswater (Glencoyne) and Helvellyn. Instead of spending the summer round remote crags, it is returning to a woodland life. Afforestation came too late to save the polecat, which was destroyed by trapping. Several recent claims were feral dark fitchew-ferrets, though there is a chance that reintroductions may establish themselves. Another absentee, the dormouse, prefers hazel woods. Myxomatosis reduced but failed to eradicate the alien rabbit, abundant enough in Cumberland back in 1621 for nets and ferrets to be used against it on the Naworth estate.

Badgers continue to survive, despite badger-digging. At Easter 1969 human enemies dug both adult and cub out of a breeding chamber on the side of Loughrigg Fell, about 1,000ft above Ellers. From Row in the Lyth Valley we followed badger tracks through the spring flora of Whitbarrow Wood to the top of Scout Scar reserve, where a massive badger colony occupies the brackeny north shoulder, its badgers crawling beneath the gate to cross the rocks. Beyond the muddy wallow of roe and red deer on the edge of the wood, where deer had nibbled young trees (even yew and juniper), we examined two old stone pits, sunk 4½ft deep behind the woodland wall, and concluded they had once been used to trap badgers or foxes coming through a hole in the bottom of the wall.

To the forests we owe the success of Lakeland's big game, even if at Thirlmere and Grizedale some reds prefer to lie out on the tops by day and come down to valley and forest to feed at night. Martindale deer range over the fells from Shap to Kentmere, occasionally swimming Ullswater and visiting Glencoyne and Gowbarrow by crossing Helvellyn range. Martindale red deer stray to Ambleside, High Wray and Furness, and east and north of Windermere from Staveley and Gill Head to Cartmel Fell, Gummer How, Whitbarrow, Strickland Hill, and even to Forest Hall, Kendal. Bavarian stags were introduced at Gowbarrow in the eighteenth century.

Big forest stags, such as those found at Grizedale, weigh between 18 and 23 stones, and hinds 10–12 stones, and in 1957 antlers measuring 35¼in long and 27¼in in girth were taken at Ellwood. Manchester Corporation killed off the large Bampton deer formerly in Naddle Forest. The Greythwaite stock of reds, to be seen from Sawry to Newby Bridge and even in the Rusland Valley in evening, developed a good weight and massive antlers, the heaviest being a fourteen-pointer weighing 28 stone 7lb in 1934. Their antlers have a spread of up to 33in and were possibly improved by a crossing with a female wapiti formerly introduced to Belle Isle in Windermere. Descendants of carted red deer from the Oxenholme Hunt visit woods from Silverdale and Arnside to Leighton Hall and Hutton Roof. Some of Lowther's former red deer are also dispersed over the fells. A Westmorland stag from Sedgwick in 1927 had antlers 39¾in long and of 32¼in span.

Roe deer thrive in conifer plantations bordered by arable land, where they feed after dark. They are widely distributed from Floriston and Wetheral beyond Carlisle to Silverdale and Furness, and from Windermere to Hoff Lunn at Appleby and Barron Wood at Kirkby Lonsdale, and include the descendants of Austrian importations to Belle Isle in 1913. Fewer inhabit the central area, where there are less conifer woods, except for modern extensions at Bassenthwaite, Elterwater, Cockermouth, Greystoke and Lowther.

Page 89 (above) Introduced greylag geese have become naturalised in most of the Lake District; this pair are nesting on an islet on Derwentwater; (below) their nest

Page 90 (*above*) The roseate tern showing its very long tail-streamers, a summer visitor to Morecambe Bay; (*below*) Sandwich terns at Drigg Point ternery showing the frequently white-speckled forehead

Roe do not travel in herds like red deer, or leave the trees before dusk. They favour the woods on Cartmel Fell, Tower Wood on the east of Lake Windermere, and Cunsey on the west, and drop fawns in Backbarrow Wood at Newby Bridge to the south. The antlers of a Whitbarrow buck in 1940 were 11$\frac{1}{16}$in long, those from another at Belle Isle in Windermere in 1918 measured 10$\frac{5}{8}$in, and a 1961 specimen from Cartmel 10$\frac{5}{16}$in. Lakeland bucks weigh about 56lb, does 41-6lb—slightly smaller than Bronze Age remains. They use dense thickets and hardwoods to protect them from cold wind and frost.

Even shyer, whistling Manchurian sika deer, with paler antlers than reds, stray from Gisburn Forest into south Lakeland woods. They have interbred with closely related reds at Cartmel to produce fertile spotted hinds, but these were shot, like the sika, to preserve the purity of the red deer. In 1969 a roe at Tower Wood, Windermere, had twin fawns, buck and doe, which visited a friend's bungalow on quiet Sunday afternoons. Fallow deer, like jackdaws, thrive in country parks where there are old and scattered deciduous trees, and few have established themselves in the wild for long.

Birds
Birdlife has profited from afforestation. The black grouse is now to be seen occasionally from Shap to Cartmel, Rusland, Hoff Lunn (Appleby), Whitbarrow, and regularly between Brantwood and Grizedale, and at Greystoke, Stainmore, Belah Gorge-Barras in north Westmorland and on the lower Pennine slopes as far north as Bewcastle. Buzzards have at least 40 breeding sites in Lakeland, mostly forest. Hen-harriers nest in the Northumberland border forest (Kielder). Siskins (Grizedale) and sometimes crossbills are induced to remain and breed. Fifty young capercaillie were hatched from 52 eggs introduced to Grizedale from Moray, but like 40 Reeve's pheasant put down there, they tend to roam away altogether. Hawfinches occupy deciduous woods like the Eden Valley, Netherby, Bassenthwaite, Windermere, Coniston and Woodwell at Silverdale. Chaffinches

F

are the commonest woodland songbirds, especially among birch and sessile oak scrub. The felling of their nesting-sites has proved a serious handicap to herons, whose heronries are formed near fishing waters. They have been built at Dallam Park (Miln-thorpe), and Lingholme (Derwentwater) with outliers at Yew-tree Tarn and near Blelham (deserted later), Smardale Mill near Kirkby Stephen, Underfield (Greenodd), Rusland Moss, Eden-hall, Muncaster Castle, and elsewhere. I investigated one heronry in the Great Wood at Corby Castle by the lower Eden in May 1954 in spite of the fact that the national census of heronries had just pronounced it extinct! Rookeries thrive in lowland trees near arable land. Blackcap warblers are common from Winder-mere to Holker, marsh and willow tits occur widely and long-tailed tits are fairly common. Tree-creepers feed their young behind bark in many woodland trees from Corby to Silverdale, but the nuthatch has only slowly colonised the southern woods. Woodcock and great spotted woodpeckers live in most forests, especially with dead birches, and the green woodpecker began its steady and noisy increase (which now includes Bassen-thwaite) in wooded southern valleys during World War II. The lesser spotted woodpecker reaches its northern limits, with just a few birds, at places like Arnside, Silverdale (Hawes Water), etc. Tree pipits are common, especially in scattered sessile oak woods.

Butterflies and Moths
From purple-hairstreak butterflies and the Welsh wave at Roud-sea and Burn Barrow woods to the Duke of Burgundy and the clouded magpie at Eggerslack Wood, butterflies and moths have many haunts. Modern mercury vapour lamp traps attract many more moths than did pre-war 'sugaring' expeditions. These traps not only catch rarities, but show the abundance of troublesome kinds like the spring brindled beauty. Butterflies flourish among the varied flora of the southern limestone woods and open country, and around Grange moth species include bordered straw, plain wave, mullein wave, small blood vein,

latticed heath, copper underwing, mottled pug, shaded pug, white satin, scarce prominent, nut-tree tussock, hedge rustic, and marbled coronet. Four-spotted footman, silver hook, red sword-grass and glaucous shears are to be found at Holker, the purple-bordered gold and the brown muslin at Meathop. The crimson-streaked snout ranges from Windermere and Keswick to Holker Moss, the small brindled beauty from Penrith to Holker, and the netted carpet from Ambleside and Windermere's Ferry House to Belle Grange in association with the spotted yellow balsam.

Barred carpet and the scarce dagger are to be seen at Wither-slack, one of the southernmost haunts of the galium carpet, a Highland moth. The brindled ochre seeks the cow parsnip round Windermere, Kendal and Penrith, the northern drab feeds on the oaks round Keswick, and the orange sallow is to be met at Windermere, where the blossom underwing seeks oak, birch and poplar in June. In 1954, mottled-umber moth larvae, aided by the little oak tortrix and small ermines, stripped the foliage from many deciduous woods round Windermere, Cartmel, and Skelwith, even including bilberry ground flora.

The spring sunshine brings forth the brimstone butterflies among the primroses on the limestone from Grange to Greenodd. Later holly blues appear in the Winster Valley. But the brown hairstreak seems to have deserted the Prunus trees at Grange and Arnside, and like the wood white and the grizzled skipper (formerly at Arnside and Silverdale), it may be extinct in Lakeland. The northernmost range of the high brown and speckled wood is the southern limestone at Witherslack, but they are seldom found. The northern brown moth swarms on Arnside Knott in August and the saxon moth ranges from Brantwood at Conis-ton to Newby Bridge.

Plants

The ground flora is inhibited by the shading foliage and acid needles of close pine forests, but it thrives in the thinner hardwoods, particularly on the limestone (as Roudsea illustrates).

Man has introduced spring snowflake in Derwentwater woods; fly honeysuckle in woods at Coniston, Windermere, Lindale (Cartmel), and Middlebarrow (Silverdale); and *Lilium pyrenaicum* in Waterslack Wood. Laburnum grows wild, an unusual event, in some woods at Keswick. The shrub *Leycestria formosa* has been introduced to Eggerslack Woods and the lower slopes of Whitbarrow Scar. Woodland orchids thrive on the limestone—long-leaved helleborine at Grange and Arnside, red helleborine and bird's-nest orchid from Arnside Knott to Silverdale Quarry, and fly orchids in several Arnside–Silverdale woods and at Haverbrack. Yellow cow wheat grows in the woodland drive at Lodore, as do different blues of Jacob's ladder in Middlebarrow Wood at Silverdale and of alkanet in Lowther Wood at Pudey Bridge, east of Kendal. Solomon's seal appears at Arnside as well, and green hellebore there and in Gaitbarrow Wood. A large colony of *Asarum europeum* is one uncommon sight in a wood at Bassenthwaite.

Twayblade is not uncommon around Grasmere, *Corydalis solida* grows in Newlands Dale, and mountain-currant bushes grow in woods north to Cumwhitton. Other plants have escaped from cultivation but still flourish, like the sensitive fern *Onoclea sensibilis* at Colton-in-Furness and elsewhere; pink *Daphne mezereum* in woods near Carlisle, Penrith, Whitbarrow and Silverdale; white butterbur at Pelter Bridge near Rydal and by the Greta at Keswick; and the equally white, but later, Japanese butterbur at Bennethead, Ullswater, and Brathay Bridge, Ambleside. The ferns in the limestone southern woods are still dug up by dealers and cultivators, one of whom told me that Warton Crag provided him with most of the crested variations he displayed at Southport Show for many years.

Bird and mammal watchers appreciate the extra warmth and cover provided by a wood, especially at dawn in winter, and a bird-feeding table there, or food placed regularly on a tree stump, is even more rewarding than in the garden. Salt-licks, even rock salt hung from a bough, become known to deer, and they will not scent you if they are upwind. Few carnivores can resist trails rubbed with old fish to end at one's observation hide, certainly not pine marten or fox. In one garden near Windermere a badger visiting the bird-table at night rang a bell in the observer's bedroom, and she could get up and photograph it. The co-evolution of red squirrel, crossbill and pine tree, of brimstone butterfly and buckthorn, moths and their food plants enables one to appreciate the need for conserving a fauna's habitat. The wood becomes more meaningful, a less lonely place, not to be destroyed for building bungalows or trampled down to bare earth.

One May morning I returned to a wood near Carlisle, a spot where I had always found roe, after many years' absence: its heart had been torn out by a timber-merchant's tractor. I saw a pair of roe that had left the wood and crossed to the remnants of an old haystack near a field-gate; the doe was heavy with young and doubly wary. A farm dog attacked her, but before he could be called off, the cornered buck met him, snorting and stamping, his small stout antlers more than a match for the collie. I mention this as an example of how wildlife clings to its old haunts. If we are to conserve species, we must preserve their territories.

CHAPTER SIX

Open Fellsides

OPEN WINDY MOORS where clouds sail the long horizon, where the quivering call of the curlew is heard all summer, and coppiced oaks glorify October and November, are the fell-walker's delight. The winter is severe. Only the Pennine Trough of Bowland is wetter than Furness, and on the Pennine border a hill farmer may lose 1,000 ewes in hard weather that takes unrecorded toll of hares and deer. In few places is the coming of spring more exhilarating. In March curlews' cries in descending flight mark new nesting territories, while the last whooper swans are still resting on the trout-tarns. One day the skylarks will be soaring in song, and the next will bring snow, forcing the birds to flock again. The strong helm-wind blowing from north or north-east in March or April may crack the earliest grouse eggs on low frosty moors, but next day sunshine and a speedwell-blue sky will thaw the frozen sheep-grazings until, at noon, one sinks ankle deep into sphagnum and cotton-grass bogs under the cries of crows and lapwings. Cartmel, Lazonby and Bolton (Hethergill) Fells are typical of such scenes.

Ardent Ruskinians make Brantwood a pilgrimage in Coniston's beautiful corner of Lakeland. From dawn until after dusk, the fells give one a sensation of solitude, though one may encounter a roe picking her nervous way along the edge of the plantations, and pied flycatcher and redstart feed their young in holes in trees above the eastern shore.

One may climb up Yewdale Beck while the buzzard from Harry Guards Wood circles overhead and pearl-bordered fritillary butterflies flutter in courtship, and turn away from Langdale to eat one's sandwiches at the top of Tilberthwaite Ghyll in the company of ravens from Lingmoor or Dow Crag. Across the slopes of Wetherlam come the whistles of ring-ouzels and on nearby High Fell is the peregrine. One may cross Coniston Moor, with its flowering bogbean and scaly stagshorn clubmoss, resident since the Ice Ages, and slide down Yewdale Crags to follow the beck into Coniston, meeting its dippers on the edge of the village. An otter came to the lake here one night to eat a pike in the reedbed.

The moor has many moods, however, and only the meteorologists enjoy those in June when the Atlantic clouds keep 'dropping a shower', and we have to keep draining the endless rain from our ears and extricating ourselves from flush bogs. Such weather makes us realise how tough the red grouse has to be, though, following such weather, we have found young lapwings and grouse dead—unable to survive more than thirty hours of cold and wet below 60° F.

Miles of purple and mauve heath and heather stretch between Finsthwaite and Greythwaite. One feels the breath of it with the north-west wind in one's face. Ahead lies a scramble of peaks. Few red grouse, woodcock or badgers live here, but the trees are noisy with jays and green woodpeckers, and the cat-cry of the buzzard drifts down from the sky over Cartmel Fell. A pair of buzzards were mating at Windermere's Gyllhead reservoir on 8 May 1972. Vipers are seen occasionally at Witherslack, High Nibthwaite, Leighton and Grizedale and grass snakes from Grizedale to Roudsea Wood.

Autumn flowers vary little on the volcanic slates: the purple heads of devil's-bit scabious, the yellow of cow wheat and goldenrod in woods, red wood-betony, white hemp nettles, blue harebells hanging low in dry places, and the purple ling across the moors.

The southern purse-web spider *Atypus affinis* and the little March-flying oak beauty moth belong to the Silverdale-Arnside limestone. Dark red helleborine grows at Warton Crag quarry, pyramid orchid at Blea Tarn, Warcrop.

Mammals

The names of many fells reveal their long association with British mammals. There is the 2,300ft Wild Boar Fell between Kirkby Stephen and Sedbergh, and Hindscarth, the pass of the hinds, in Newlands Valley. Judging by the number of homes historians have found for the last wolf in England, it had more lives than the proverbial cat. Wolfa, which claims the 'kill' of the last wolf of Inglewood Forest on Humphrey Head, may have been a place for the annual payment of wolves' heads, or more likely named from the man who built his homestead there. Ulpha, the wolf-hollow or trap, may have been wolf-haga or fence. The wolf's Scandinavian name *ulfr* appears in Uldale, Ullock Pike on Skiddaw and Ullscarf Pike, the pass of the wolf, at the Head of Borrowdale. Gummers How is a corruption of Gimmers How, the sheep's hill, but Cat Bells is as likely derived from *Quatre Belles*, a bevy of local ladies, as from the wild cat's bield or shelter.

Short-tailed field voles, commonest of the mammals, provide prey for foxes, pine martens, buzzards, barn owls, kestrels and short-eared owls, and have themselves prospered under afforestation. Lean meadow hares range much higher than the fields, and mountain hares wander from the Cheviots. Weasels and stoats, brown and bloodthirsty, hunt the voles and leverets of the fellside. Roosting wrens or yellowhammers, larks or meadow pipits, will rise in alarm from the path of the stoat worming its way across the ground soon after daybreak. Even the short-eared owl is quick to release the 5oz of animated fury when it mistakenly seizes a weasel. Yet hare or rabbit with young will sometimes drive off stoat or weasel.

In 1957 Blencathra Hounds roused a pine marten at the boulder-strewn foot of Carrock Crag near Mungrisdale. Such an interesting animal can also be expected among the invigorating winds at the dale head of Kentmere and the nearby Troutbeck from Windermere, as well as at Riggindale above Mardale, Eskdale, Wasdale, Ennerdale, Borrowdale, Martindale, Patterdale, Dunnerdale–Coniston and Grayrigg Hause to Tebay above Lunesdale.

Red deer are encountered on many fells, especially between Angle Tarn beyond Patterdale and High Street, with herds on the Nab above Ullswater, but their range overlaps forest and dale.

Every hand is raised against the fox because of the 8 per cent or so of poultry sometimes included in his prey. He will take a young lamb where a ewe with twins is occupied guarding one of them, yet ewes have been seen butting away the fox trying to reach their singleton. Fell foxes almost never attack adult sheep, as the big Grampian or Cheviot foxes may do in severe weather. Where rabbits are plentiful they form up to 44 per cent of a fox's diet, and many foxes eat up to 4,000 mice or voles a year, with other small rodents—or lizards—added. Carrion sheep or deer after winter snows will comprise around 8 per cent of diet in Lakeland, and the large amount of grass eaten characterises the droppings. The remainder ranges from beechmast and blackberries to fallen apples. Canine distemper and hepatitis are more often spread by stray dogs than by foxes, and hardpad is more often found in badgers.

Foxes are not deliberately introduced in Lakeland to improve the strain, or put down for sport as in the English Midlands, though cubs from the fells have been sold to southern hunts. Hunting, which lasts from the end of September to mid-May, will never rid the area of foxes, unless it kills more than 75 per cent of the population, which it cannot. Neither bounties nor illegal strychnine will check them as long as their habitat remains attractive: woodlands with thick cover, or the margins of farmland with rough fields and brushwood on well-drained soil. Their high death-rate is countered by a high birth-rate, despite a short breeding season in February or early March.

The vixen's ghoulish scream marks her oestrous, from mid-December to late February. Daily fighting with forepaws on each other's shoulders marks out the dominant before the mating season begins, when pairing progresses from daily fights or passive whining between dog and vixen to tolerance, premating behaviour and finally constant companionship. Mating probably takes place mostly at night, but occasionally it may be seen on the fells on late February mornings, nearly a month later than in southern England. The usual litter is four, though two vixens may share an earth.

Because den areas are often not the hunting areas, a farmer may rightly tell you of foxes not killing prey near their dens. Flat-furred in winter and handsome in the ruffled upstanding fur of spring, when he starts moulting, the fox is worth watching at any time. Fell foxes frequently weigh up to 20lb, though the average is around 15lb, and measure more than 4ft nose to tag. Lakeland terriers do not have it all their own way when put down a bield to bolt the fox: I have been shown one blinded when a fox seized it by the face which was still bolting foxes, and occasionally a terrier is killed underground.

Birds

Times have changed since partridge-killing records from the 4,000 acre Netherby estate by the Border Esk were more important than scientific studies and bird-counts on the fells. There are still moors from Penrith, Kettlepot, Stowgill, Bowes Moor, etc, to Muncaster Castle where husky-voiced red grouse flap their wings against the ground and try to lure one from their chicks, escaping on woolly brown legs, their down dappled like fruit cake. In the 1960s eight guns shot 275 brace in four days at Geltsdale on the Cumberland–Northumbriand border and six guns killed 122½ brace at Knipe in Westmorland. Walking-up is general on the high sheep moors of Westmorland, such as Long Sleddale (Kendal), Kirkby Moor (Ulverston), Shap, Lowther, and Brackenbank (Lazonby) on Burnhope. There are black grouse on the Durham border, at Killhope in Cumberland, and on Ousby moor. At dusk the cock partridge flies to roost; calling up his covey to leave no trail. Their roosts, where they settle tails together, are marked by droppings, like those of grouse.

Stone walls zigzagging their dry way across the fells provide nesting niches for redstart and wheatear. Uplands like Stainmore Common, above Brough, are visited by hen-harriers, which nest sometimes on the east Westmorland and Northumberland border. Hunted by the dashing merlin, little meadow pipits themselves eat craneflies, whose hatch also attracts black-headed gulls from the tarns and rooks from the dales. Meadow pipits have nested in the wall-cavity of a roofless building on the Westmorland fells. Carrion crows nest up to 1,500ft.

Buzzards are still shot illegally, a sad reflection on the limited education or experience of squire or shooting tenant, for they prey upon small rodents and ground beetles, not birds. Formerly as many nested on rock ledges and in quarries as in trees, but increased rock-climbing has caused more of them to renovate old crows' nests, such as one in a rowan on Souther fell in Mungrisdale, north of Troutbeck, a few years ago, others nesting at Cartmel, Greythwaite, Grizedale, etc. High Street and Riggindale's golden eagles fly across Martindale Nab to feed young hatched in June.

About eighty pairs of curlew nest on the north Lancashire fells such as Clough Pike, Harris End, Grizedale and Whitbarrow Scar, and forty pairs in south Westmorland. The brimstone-and-treacle plumage of the yellowhammer is a familiar fellside sight wherever bracken grows. There have been albinos in the Eden Valley and at Plumpton. Ring-ouzels occasionally enter Cumbrian fell woods, where they inhabit the rocky slopes above 1,000ft. The cirl bunting, like the lesser whitethroat, reaches its northern limit here, but continues to decline, probably for climatic reasons. Nightjars have also declined, though a few occupy the heaths near Beacon Hill, the Rusland Valley and Penrith. Two pairs of golden plover are usually resident on Skiddaw and another pair on Deepdale Common, but, like dunlin, they prefer the Pennine moors. A few dunlin and several golden plover nest on Tailbridge and Stainmore Commons, the former a 100 acre peat-bog near Kirkby Stephen.

The skylark is undoubtedly the busiest songbird of the low

moor, leading the dawn chorus and continuing after sunset. I have noted it singing on 222 and 247 days in a year, compared to 237 and 266 by the woodland song thrush, 199 and 143 by the yellowhammer, 153 and 145 by the chaffinch, 132 and 133 by the mistle thrush and 176 and 209 by the blackbird. Like the meadow pipit, its aerial song is heard around 1,000ft. In winter both birds flock and leave the exposed fellsides until spring, but returning down Mickleden at dusk at the end of one October I flushed a few still roosting in the rushes. In spring the vehement cock skylark often sings from a clod with a commanding view, and at night he has been found roosting on such a clod, not far from the incubating hen bird. Tree pipits, yellowhammers and redstarts are characteristic of the lower slopes, often with whin-chats, linnets and, above the trees, meadow pipits.

The return of lapwings to the fellside is a sign of spring. Once a flock of lapwings, including one ringed above Ullswater, were blown from Britain to Newfoundland but it was an accidental journey which overshot their more normal Irish wintering grounds, where the weather is milder. Like the pine woods, the open fell can be almost devoid of birdlife in hard winter weather, except around the hill farmsteads. The lapwing does not breed commonly above 1,200ft, or upon steep or brackeny slopes. In hard weather vast flocks of lapwings and curlews from the fells resort to Morecambe Bay, where conditions are milder. Whinchats are also fellside visitors in spring.

One February 130 siskins were counted among the alders and other trees near Heights Farm on Cartmel Fell (by Allen Airey).

Insects

Ground and heather beetles, moths and migrating butterflies form much of the insect life. The bog bush-cricket *Platycleis* (*Metrioptera*) *brachyptera* has been found on Wan Fell, but there are no field crickets or, apparently, mole crickets. The common green grasshopper *viridulus* appears in June, as does the field grasshopper *brunneus*. Often identified by stridulation alone, these are varied by the mottled *maculatus* and the meadow *parallelus* on Wan Fell, near Great Salkeld.

Antler-moth caterpillars sometimes strip the herbage on Skiddaw, and buff ermines once stripped acres of bracken near Buttermere, normally food of broom moths. Emperor, fox and oak eggar are more attractive insects on the fells, either assembling to the scent of the female carried in a box as one walks along, or appearing as handsome caterpillars, as does the hairy brown fox moth, so conspicuous later on. Northern wave and dart moths range from Skiddaw to Moor House in east Westmorland in July. Grey mountain carpets are common on the higher fells, and the galium carpet, similar to its Highland form, has its southernmost British haunt at Witherslack as well as inhabiting Cliburn Moss in the Upper Eden Valley, away from the mountains. The yellow-ringed carpet follows the white meadow saxifrage over Lakeland. The olive moth, like the dingy skipper butterfly, ranges from Grange and Kendal to Hutton Roof. Ringlet butterflies favour Orton in summer and are rarer near Leighton. Grayling butterflies flutter over many Westmorland and north Lancashire fells, Haworth's little carpet moth and the heath rivulet appearing near Grange-over-Sands also. The northern argent and sable haunts the bilberry hills near Carlisle, and the pale oak eggar is on the moors near Kendal.

Among butterflies, a larger darker form of Scotch argus is found on damp and grassy hillsides. Brimstones, holly blues and Duke of Burgundies in spring, graylings, blues, purple hairstreaks and four or five kinds of fritillary in summer, are attracted to the silver-grey limestones. From Eggerslack's cowslips and primroses, the Duke of Burgundy ranges north to Kendal. Violets in Holker's Roudsea Wood attract brown fritillaries, and its old pines the white satin-carpet moths, while purple hairstreaks favour the oaks at Burn Barrow Wood. Large and dingy skippers flit about Cartmel Fell. In summer we see dark green fritillaries at Hampsfell, Eggerslack and Yewbarrow.

Collectors have taken a heavy toll of Massey's variety of silver-studded blue butterfly from Meathop and Witherslack.

Plants

The grassy fells have much of botanical interest, like the fragrant and frothy flowers of spignel meum near the Shap Road, at the reservoir site at Wet Sleddale, in a field near Torver (Coniston), in Grayrigg Forest and Common and by the roadside at Dillicar Common, Tebay. Rigid buckler and hard shield ferns enjoy the southern limestone pavement fells. Seventeen species of orchid and some 700 flowering plants flourish on the carboniferous limestone round Arnside and Silverdale. In addition to dog, hairy and sweet violets, creamy-white *rupestris*, once considered exclusive to Teesdale's Widdybank Fell, grows on the grassy top of Arnside Knott among hairy violets and carlines facing inland (and on Long Fell, also in Westmorland), differing in colour and habit from the same species 7 miles away in Teesdale. Lower down grow whitebeam, buckthorn and spindle trees; at the top junipers and rock-roses; with dark red helleborine on its steeper southern slope opposite the tower. The dwarf burnt orchid *ustula* grows here, from Black Dyke to Silverdale Moss. The leaves of deadly nightshade (a seashore plant here, too) are eaten by the small beetle *Epitrix atropa*. Green hellebore grows by the Black Dyke path from the Arnside road to the Tower, as well as on the Knott and in Silverdale's Middlebarrow Wood and Hagg Wood, and its variety *occidentalis* grows in a meadow below the Knott. Buckthorn is here with brimstone butterflies. Western spiked speedwell appears at Arnside Park and Far Arnside. Baneberry is common in the woods round the Tower, along with lily-of-the-valley and hartstongue, and the slopes of Castle Barrow are covered with dropworts, columbines and hairy violets.

The best fells for flowers (and Lepidoptera) are in fact the southern limestones. Pink bird's-eye primrose ranges from Silverdale to Rydal, Swindale, Windermere and Loughrigg.

From Row in the Lyth valley it is but a gentle wood slope up by Whitbarrow's spring primroses, early purple orchids, morelle mushrooms and wild arums to the exposed summit of Scout Scar, where lizards bask in summer sunshine among limestone crevices harbouring polypody, green spleenwort and moon-wort ferns below the juniper bushes. The fell is flanked with banks of leafless yellow bird's-nest flower (*Monotropa*) under hazel, and bird's-nest orchid; of purple broad-leaved and marsh helleborine orchids; and frog, fly, fragrant, twayblade and greater and lesser butterfly orchids. Hoary and common rock-roses decorate the limestone with yellow, along with tiny squinancy wort further north than Arnside, which is said to be its northernmost location in Europe. Ramblers sometimes con-fuse horseshoe and kidney vetches with birdsfoot trefoil here. Mountain everlasting, traveller's joy, lily-of-the-valley, buck-thorn, herb paris, rue-leafed saxifrage, bloody cranesbill, colum-bine and many others grow in the striking calcicole flora. Mountain bedstraw, *sterneri*, appears near Underbarrow Scar, another limestone haunt.

Great white butterfly orchid grows at Endmoor and School Knott near Windermere, and among the whitebeam trees on the western side of Whitbarrow and Cunswick Scar there is local pride in the variety *lancastriense*, which has narrower, more obtuse leaves, with veins less prominent and greyer underhairs. But others consider it a segregate or variation of the common *aria*. Large-leaved lime grows in Barrowfield woods, and Solomon's seal, herb paris, *Daphne mezereum* and narrow-leafed helleborine in Brightseer Woods, where the lady's slipper once reached its westernmost extent. There are several stands of forked spleenwort, but doubts over bristle fern surviving in Westmorland.

Arnside is associated with the localised Breckland sedge *eri-cetorum*, with carline thistle, columbine, lily-of-the-valley, lesser dandelion, mouse-eared hawkweed, squinancy wort between the Tower and Hazelslack, fields of ox-eyes, and frequent fly orchids by the path on Arnside Knott and towards Silverdale.

The latter's enduring attraction is also its limestone flora. The quarry wood above Leighton Moss has bird's-nest orchid by its roadside steps and, in the quarry noisy with jackdaws, in June 1972, 107 fly orchids were counted in one corner of the quarry and a dozen dark red or purple helleborines were counted another year among yellow rock-roses, broad-leaved helleborines and common spotted orchids. There were lesser butterfly and lesser twayblade orchids as well as deadly nightshade and great knapweed there. Middlebarrow Fell wood is graced with angular and common Solomon's seals, herb paris, hundreds of twayblade orchids and lilies-of-the-valley, as well as dogwood, purging buckthorn, whitebeam, wild service tree and spurge laurel, while green hellebore and deadly nightshade grow outside, and *Lilium pyrenaicum* was naturalised here.

Woodcock nest here and at Hazelwood, and near the nature trail in Eaves Wood, grow spurge laurel and herb paris. Waterslack, which is all part of one great wooded fellside belonging to the National Trust, shelters bird's-nest orchid and broadleaved helleborines, spindle, juniper and cut-leafed geranium. One also sees acres of lily-of-the-valley mixed with columbines, rock-roses, mountain melic-grass, fingered sedge, Solomon's seal, hartstongues, herb paris, and, in the limestone cleats near the Pepper Pot on the summit, dark red helleborines, junipers and black-stalked spleenwort ferns. Stone bramble is common on these hillsides, and the greenish-yellow fenland variety of blue Sesleria, *luteoalba*, grows on the north slope of Arnside Knott.

The yew trees of Arnside Park attract cole tits in winter to feed on their red fruits, and the southern wood-ants' hillocks of pine needles are a feature. Rigid buckler is a typical fern on the limestone pavements from Whitbarrow and Scout Scar to Great Ashby Scar, Wild Boar Fell, north of Sunbiggin Tarn, Brough (Hillbeck), Honister Crag, Warton Crag and Hutton Roof to Farleton Knot.

These limestone hills harbour it on Arnside Knot and the Fairy Steps to the limestone-pavement clints at Slack Head, to

Page 107 (above) An oystercatcher on a typical shingle nest just above high-tide mark. There is a small nesting population, but large flocks of immigrant birds winter in the area; (below) black guillemots which now nest on St Bees Head

Page 108 (*above*) A male natterjack toad, marked by its yellow dorsal-line, distends its throat in its spring mating cry; although once common on brackish southern estuaries, it now has few haunts left; (*below*) the violet ground beetle, a useful predator in the dales

the east of Arnside, where Underlaid Wood, Hazelslack and Arnside Moss introduce one to more herb paris, lilies-of-the-valley and the diminishing wild daffodils, once common in all the woods to Silverdale. Bloody cranesbill, rock-rose and spring cinquefoil colour the rocks and the cowslips in the meadows mix with early purple and green-winged meadow orchids. Gromwell grows in a copse here. Bird cherry and spindle typify the trees of the limestone near the Steps and the Old Wood below Slack Head. Baneberry, a white flower among the herb paris and others in Middlebarrow and other woods, grows no further south.

Silverdale is a haunt of fragrant orchids, frog orchids, dropworts, and rare yellow star-of-Bethlehem, and there are magnificent clusters of snowdrops between Crag Wood and the copper mines at Warton, an old haunt of the brown argus. Its gently rolling hills are wooded thickly with deciduous trees, where green woodpeckers call and great bellflower rises in stately splendour. Its limestones are bright with rock-rose, and squinancy wort's tiny pink flowers dot the grass towards Arnside, where there are ponds with water soldier. Its wet woods encrusted with lichen lead to limestone pavements north of the station, with limestone polypody, rigid buckler, prickly shield and hartstongue among a wealth of ferns. We have not seen its pyramid and small burnt orchids recently.

Alpine cinquefoil grows here, as well as on Helvellyn Crags. The absence of grazing on the limestone saddle of Hutton Roof at 900ft, and on Dalton Fell and Farleton Crags and Holme-park, which dominate the eastern skyline between Burton-in-Kendal and Kirkby Lonsdale, has allowed a rich flora to grow up in the open glades of limestone pavement between the spruce plantations at the foot of the crags—darkened helleborine orchid, rigid buckler, limestone polypody, angular Solomon's seal, herb paris and lesser meadow rue among the yews and junipers. Birdsfoot sedge, a dry grassland calcicole at its northernmost British range in Lakeland, grows on Hutton Roof and on Whitbarrow and Cunswick Screes. Blue moor grass and moun-

G

tain melic are everywhere. The rare Pennine milkwort *amara* was noted on Orton Scar limestone above Tebay.

Over 400 plants may be found in flower within 4 miles of Grange-over-Sands in spring, as well as seventeen ferns, one of which is the *Ceterach*.

Orton Fell, south of Shap, is a historic site of alpine *Bartsia*, and shares with Great Ashby isolated sites of perennial flax, bird's-eye primrose and birdsfoot sedge. Northern water forget-me-not *brevifolia* grows on the Kendal side of Howter Fell and Cross Fell, and alpine forget-me-not on Mickle Fell. Alpine *Saussurea* appears on the fells above Windermere, where the soil creeps gradually down to the dales, along with the purple small scabious. After staying one September night in a cottage overlooking Coniston, I found my host had decorated my breakfast table with meadow saffron, gathered from an old colony introduced on a hillside towards Hawkshead. It also grows near Finsthwaite and in Cumberland, near Keswick.

CHAPTER SEVEN

Dales

A GREEN DALE carved by widening glaciers from the mountains provides a corridor by which spring and summer bird-migrants may penetrate the heart of Lakeland. Some of the stream-fed valleys are discussed in Chapter 8 on rivers. Several are lakeless, like Swindale, Long Sleddale, Dunnerdale and Eskdale, but most are threaded by trout streams. Their mildness and greenness contrasts with seemingly bleak bare mountains, for retreating glaciers left boulder clay and eroded rock-dust to make their fertile soil, and alluvial deposits were added later. Richly contrasting valleys radiate from Scafell and the Pike, and flank the peaks of Great Gable and Bowfell.

Ornamented with oak, ash and birch woods, and underplanted with hosts of hybrid rhododendrons that thrive in the rain, their country parks are stocked with a predators' banquet of alien pheasants. Their luxurious gardens, occasionally opened to the public, are protected from wind and passing traffic, and, in consequence, bloom magnificently. Here the botanist finds uncommon foreign trees and shrubs thriving in the wet but sheltered conditions.

Around Ullswater in July one may observe the beginnings of the autumn passage from Scotland of adult and immature common gulls, which have spent the night roosting on the lake, though plenty of eggs and chicks still remain in their northern colonies. At dawn the green of Matterdale is enlivened by ravens, still tumbling in aerial display as if it were spring, but at Glencoyne wood, Glenridding, friendly pied flycatchers, like the gulls, are beginning migration.

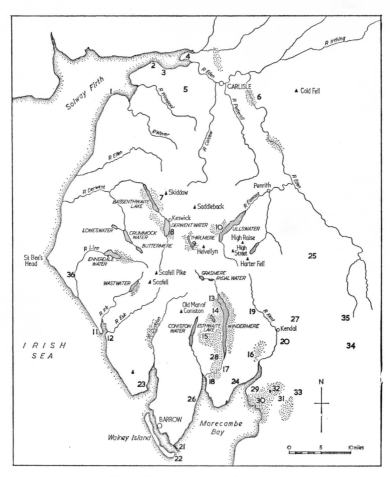

Fig 6   Nature reserves and preserves

KEYS TO MAP OPPOSITE

1. Grune Point (birds and plants)
2. Bowness-on-Solway gravelpits (LNT)
3. Glasson Moss (NC), 140 acres
4. Rockliffe Marsh (LNT)
5. Bucknell Fell, Orton (LNT)
6. Wetheral Woods (NT), 21 acres
7. Ivy Crag Wood, Under Skiddaw, Bassenthwaite (LNT), (plants)
8. Derwentwater Islands (birds)
9. Holly Bank, Thirlmere
10. Glencoyne Wood (NT)
11. Drigg Point, Ravenglass Ternery (Cumb CC)
12. Eskmeals Dunes (LNT)
13. Blelham Tarn (NC)
14. Esthwaite North Fen (NC)
15. Grizedale Forest (Forestry Comm), 7,440 acres
16. Scout Scar (LNT), 250 acres
17. Rusland Moss (NC), 30 acres
18. Roudsea Wood (NC)
19. Dorothy Farrer's Spring, Staveley
20. Grasforth, Natland (birds)
21. Foulney Island ternery (BR)
22. South Walney Island gullery (LNT)
23. Haws Millom (greylag geese) (S Cumb Wildfowlers' Assoc)
24. Cat Crag, Meathop Moss (LNT), (ferns, etc)
25. Orton Scar, Tebay (LNT)
26. Plumpton Quarry, Ulverston (LNT), (ferns, etc)
27. Fisher Tarn, Kendal (birds)
28. Haybridge (British Deer Soc)
29. Arnside Knott (beechwood, etc), 106 acres
30. Silverdale, Eaves and Waterslack Woods (NT), 21 acres Castlebarrow, 97 acres Middlebarrow Wood, Stack Orchard (coastal wood), 15 acres
31. Leighton Hall Moss (RSPB), (birds)
32. Hawes Water (NC)
33. Hale Moss (LNT), 1 acre
34. Crosby Gill, Crosby Ravensworth (LNT)
35. Moor House (NC)
36. Egremont Wildfowlers' Assoc

Dungeon Ghyll Old Hotel at the head of Great Langdale Valley is the start of many walks up to Hell Gill above Oxendale. Overhead croak the ravens that nest on the 'Sevens' (juniper) rock above Stool End Farm, on The Bank of Mickleden, where Coniston hounds sometimes find a fox. Peregrines no longer come from their old eyrie on Blake Rigg Crag above Blea Tarn, but in 1970 the first red squirrel for seven years visited the tawny owls' few perching trees at Stool End, the topmost farm in Great Langdale and the beginning of the track to Bowfell, Crinkle Crags and Eskdale, 12 miles away. Blackheaded gulls nest among bogbean at Low Oxen Fell on the old Lancashire side of Little Langdale Tarn until autumn, and the Tarn also provides marsh clubmoss and views of mergansers nesting in summer.

To view Great Langdale at its best one should continue from Stool End up Brown Gill to the little Red Tarn between Pike O'Blisco and Crinkle Crags, 2,816ft above. A descent of a mile takes one to the climb up Bowfell's 2,960ft, with a view extending south to Coniston Old Man and Wetherlam, west across Eskdale to Scafell and east to the Langdales. One can descend via Angle Tarn and the steep Rossett Ghyll, and walk along the valley from Mickleden. Another good walk is to ascend Mill Gill from the new hotel at Dungeon Ghyll to Stickle Tarn below Pavey Ark and Harrison Stickle, then climb to 2,000ft on Blea Rigg and look north down into Easedale and south into Langdale. Thence once may move to Silver Howe's 1,292ft and down Mega Gill to Chapel Stile and Elterwater, with its mergansers.

From Ambleside to Troutbeck wild gooseberries and raspberries grow beside the road—and so much purple-blue wood geranium that one wonders why Linnaeus named it *sylvaticum*, for with yellow Welsh poppies that have escaped from cultivation it borders many Lakeland lanes and meadow-sides, yet climbs much higher to Kirkstone and Wansfell. Up Nanny Lane to Wansfell wheatears flit from rock to rock and wild strawberries ripen, and the 1,580ft summit affords a bird's-eye view of the whole coast of Morecambe Bay to Ulverston. One

may also see the length of Windermere, the frowning face of
Coniston Old Man, Langdale Pikes, the Brathay, meandering
through its vivid green valley, Wrynose Pass, Bowfell and
Scafell Pike. Below lie Ambleside, where the yellow balsam
grows, Rydal Water, Grasmere, and the Red Screes descending
to Kirkstone Pass. Behind lies the Troutbeck Valley backed by
High Street (hiding the home of the red deer of Martindale),
and the conspicuous cone of Il Bell.

Although the rock is Silurian, a few bird's-eye primroses grow
between Wansfell and Ambleside. The damp moor supports
yellow mountain saxifrage, butterworts, little marsh valerian
and lady's mantle as well as scaly *Selaginella*, the lesser clubmoss, and yellow distant sedges among the deer grass. Near
Troutbeck village one sees barberry, guelder rose, bird cherry
and berry-bearing buckthorn, which give way to great valerian,
great salad burnet, and golden saxifrage beside field drains and
to sweet woodruff, bugle, marsh woundwort, bistort and even
a few butterworts in the moister part of Nanny Lane. Among the
yellow hawkweeds, *Hieracium auranticum* has escaped from village
gardens to a field. Yellow fumitory climbs mossy walls that are
prolific at all seasons in polypody and parsley, maidenhair
spleenwort and delicate wall rue, the commonest wall fern. A
dwarf petal-less form of shepherd's purse with mauve sepals has
been found. The rain encourages male and lady ferns, mountain
fern, beech fern and broad buckler, while edible *Boletus* flourishes
among the fungi.

Mammals

Martindale, the only natural sporting deer forest in England, is
of much interest. The mixture of blood from wild Martindale
red deer and escaped park deer produced the pre-war herd.
Some 250 descendants still wander over Lakeland to Shap and
Kentmere, Helvellyn and Tebay, particularly the stags. They
return annually for the autumn rut, chiefly to the 1,888ft Nab,
which divides Bannerdale from Rampsghyll. They share Mar-

tindale with Swaledale sheep and Galloway cattle. Martindale stags average 17½ to 18 stones and hinds 14 stones, weighed with heart and liver. Larger deer used to range Naddle Forest forty years ago. Hunted into the middle of the last century, the deer here have since been stalked, with a post-World War II annual kill of ten to fifteen stags and eight to ten hinds, about half the pre-war kill. Stalking begins in late August; it is necessary to kill surplus hinds in their season.

We have followed their tracks over miles of glorious fell down to Patterdale and the plantations on the slopes of Helvellyn, losing them through the low clouds to Red Tarn and the snow of Striding Edge, for stags leave Rampside after the autumn rut. One may imitate the roar of a stag on a wooden-cased reed, and gain a fair idea of their numbers from their deep growling answers. The hind's short bark of alarm is quite different.

Around seventy years ago, Martindale deer were sometimes fed in hard winters and were not truly wild. When Oxenholme staghounds hunted carted deer before World War I, some outlying hinds bred with wild stags that came down from Martindale. By World War II Lakeland was well stocked with wild red deer ranging over an area 30 miles from east to west and 50 miles from north to south, though not all were Martindale deer. Hinchcliffe's *Backwater in Lakeland* portrays the lightly antlered heads of three Martindale stags that wandered into Mardale, which happens especially when snow lies deep in the forest.

While few red deer remain from the original herd in Lowther Park, thirty Warnham (Sussex) animals were recently introduced to Holker Park. Reduced from 2,000 acres to 730, Lowther recently acquired some thirty-five reds from Stoke Park, Badminton, and the Scottish Highlands, the same number of fallow and about eight sika from the wild. The former Lowther red stags averaged 17 stones 12lb, and the hinds 10 stones 10lb. Every few years a hummel or an antlerless stag, rare in parks, appeared. The herd probably had its origin in Martindale, with fresh blood from Warnham Court and hinds from Scotland until the last introduction from Raby (Yorkshire) in 1923. The colour of the fallow deer here was a mixture of lemon (from the Stapleford Park, Leicestershire, blood), black (from the Brougham herd), white and dappled, but the original fallow herd was killed off in 1950.

Fallow herds survive in only five parks—the light menil race at Holker and among other kinds at Dallam Tower (Milnthorpe); the dark Norman hunting race at Levens Park (Kendal); the reintroduced Lowther herd; and blackish-brown animals dappled and occasionally white at Dalemain Park (Penrith), established nearly a century ago with occasional introductions from Lowther. The herd on Dallam Park's 136 acres, enclosed in 1720, received Lowther blood in 1924. Wild roe, inhabiting woods in many dales, wander out at night, as their snow-tracks reveal.

Badgers breed in most dales, but their extensive excavations often exaggerate their number. They are often dug out and treated cruelly. Paths trodden out by their broad five-toed footprints often lead to fields where they eat a variety of food, from toads and voles to many beetles, earthworms, and even stubble oats, judging from the contents of their stomachs. As they are not named as vermin in Section 98 (3) of the 1947 Agricultural Act, it is illegal to gas them. In autumn they are largely vegetarian, but in early morning they may sometimes be seen turning cowflaights over for the grubs of yellow dung flies. Their energetic bed-making all too often reveals their breeding haunts to the terrier-man, who rudely disturbs their snoring sleep. They are not confined to wooded valleys, but range 1,000ft on to the fells. The suggestion in Macpherson's 1892 *Fauna* that 'From 1830 onwards badgers were extinct in Westmorland and Cumberland' exaggerated their former scarcity around Windermere and Cartmel. Some were reintroduced. Born 5½in long in February or March, and weighing up to 20lb by autumn, badgers start digging at about 101 days and marking the extent of their territory with anal scent-glands at about 118 days. After an earth has been used for 10 to 20 years by successive generations, it will have acquired three to eight entrances, as well as smaller air-holes. Large amounts of vitamins A and D in the fat they store mark badgers as winter-active mammals, unlike hibernators such as hedgehogs. They occupy Kentmere and Long Sleddale.

Red squirrels, woodmice and all three shrews inhabit the dales, and there are almost equal chances of meeting them abroad in winter snow. Star performers in the summer treetops, squirrel populations fluctuate with the amount of seeds produced by conifers like larch and Scots pine, the number of acorns, the increase or decrease of garden bird-feeding tables, and the severity or mildness of winters. Nut-bearing shade-trees along streamsides encourage both kinds of squirrel. Despite their attractive looks, they carry coccidiosis, though fewer external parasites than the hedgehog, whose ticks carry brucellosis (bovine contagious abortion). Farm dogs, however, are more dangerous carriers of the latter than hedgehogs, which cannot eat eggs larger than thrushes, unless already cracked—and even if they snuggle into a cow byre for warmth, they don't suck cows!

Birds

One June day when peregrines were nesting at Blue Ghyll, up Kirkstone Pass, and the ravens had long left their ravenage beyond the Red Screes, a common breeding-bird census I took of the dale at Troutbeck revealed 181 birds of 22 species. The village and farm house-sparrow was the most numerous; then came song thrush, willow warbler, blackbird, robin, chaffinch, blue tit, meadow pipit, swallow, starling, pied wagtail, house martin, great tit, redstart, mistle thrush, swift, yellowhammer, dipper (at the beck), wren, jackdaw, whitethroat, woodcock (in Elleray woods), kingfisher and cuckoo. Non-breeding herring gulls and lesser blackbacks visit the dales regularly. Heronries have been built in Deepdale, Patterdale, Smardale, Eskdale (Muncaster), Edenhall, Rusland Moss, Underfield (Greenodd), etc. One song thrush's nest I saw in Troutbeck was lined with rotted wood instead of the usual mud.

Birdlife in the dales is rich in passerines, especially pied fly-

catchers, redstarts and titmice (aided by nest-boxes). I was introduced to the Lakeland stronghold of the first-named when
dining *al fresco* in the late Dr H. J. Moon's famous pre-war
garden at Glenridding, above Patterdale. Here they descended
from nest-boxes on the trees to take scraps from the table.
They extended their nesting to the adjoining Glencoyne Woods,
beside Ullswater, where 22 of their nests were found in 2–3
acres. They nest in cottage roofs on the outskirts of Keswick,
Windermere and Ambleside, in trees by the shores of Derwentwater below Derwent Bank, and by Coniston Water, reaching
nearly 1,000ft near the Bela Viaduct under Stainmore.

Bramblings and siskins come in winter to the dales. A robin
ringed in Cumberland was found wintering in France. One
hopped on to Wordsworth's dinner table and into Dorothy's
room. Chaffinches abound in woods in spring and summer,
when the wood warbler seeks the shade. The communal roosts
of pied wagtails have ranged from the glass roof of Carlisle
railway station to willow beds by the Caldew. Yellow wagtails
nest in wet fields, especially in Long Sleddale. Sandpipers whistle
beside streams in summer, and in autumn and winter curlew
herds visit flooded fields. Quail nested in a field near Durdar
(Carlisle) during World War II, but their summer incursions are
less frequent than those of the passing corncrakes in Ennerdale.
The more sheltered southern dales have more small birds, such
as tree-sparrows round the Lyth farms and hawfinches at Silverdale (Woodwell). The green woodpecker ranges through Yewdale to Esthwaite. Crossbills, when they do come, favour the larch
woods between Ambleside and Skelwith Bridge. Jackdaws are
attracted to quarries, and over 1,000 have roosted in winter in
the woods near Meathop (Grange) after feeding on the fells.
Rookeries are closely associated with arable farms, woodcock
with woodland near soil rich in earthworms. Barn owls still
breed about farms, and one from Burneside was recovered 100
miles away in Staffordshire in its first winter. Altogether 133
species of birds have been noted in the Cleator district of Ennerdale.

Buzzards hunt the open country for its rabbits, nesting in Deepdale and lowland haunts like Foulshaw Moss farm, Holker Old Park (1954), etc. Winter sends more woodpigeons from Scotland. One shot in April in Cumberland contained 8,000 seeds weighing 4gm, including those of spreading orache, vetches and clover. I once saw a partly white woodpigeon near Carlisle.

Insects

Several of Lakeland's dozen dragonflies may be seen away from the lakes, some on the quieter pools of the beck in Yewdale. In spring and summer butterflies flourish, especially in southern limestone areas, including brimstones, brown and Scotch arguses, speckled wood, small and dingy skippers, pearl-bordered and other fritillaries, the Duke of Burgundy north to Kendal and the holly blue as far north as Carlisle. Grass supplies food for the large nutmeg moth in Eskdale.

Plants

Many plants also prefer limestone, though most dale walls are overgrown with parsley fern and spleenworts, tiny cymbalaria, and sometimes rusty-backed *Ceterach*, as at Grasmere, while yellow Welsh poppy, blue mountain-geranium and big pink foxgloves seed beside them. A rich lichen flora shows the absence of pollution. Wild daffodils or introduced hybrids follow spring snowdrops in the plantations. Plenty of field gentians grow around Mardale and Great Langdale, as does occasionally the autumn gentian; and marsh andromeda, jointed rush and lesser bladderwort appear in Mosedale. Alien Japanese butterbur, a garden outcast, has established itself by the roadside wall at Clappersgate, near Ambleside. Water avens proliferate in Borrowdale, with melancholy thistle at Watendlath and globe flower at the tarn. Bird's-eye primrose grows in a boggy dale east of Ennerdale lake, and also in Rigg Beck ravine at Kirkby Stephen, on the moors at Sunbiggin Tarn, near

Tilberthwaite Ghyll, in the valley between Rydal and Fairfield, on Rough Crag at Mardale Head and Wansfell pike, and between Arnside and Silverdale.

Rusland Moss, a raised bog named from its abundance of rushes, is not only well known for its roe and heron, but in 1961 the purple moor-grass and its sphagnum moss became Britain's first habitat for the gossamer spider *Maro lepidus*. The fells may be chin-high with summer bracken, but the connoisseur finds more variety of plantlife in damp haunts in Borrowdale, Langdale, Kentmere, Troutbeck, Silverdale-Warton Crag, and around Kendal and Coniston. Killarney or bristle fern was once found near Rydal, and the exquisite grass-of-parnassus grows at Grange-in-Borrowdale and above Windermere and Greythwaite.

The botanist should also pause in the rich gardens and parks, for their exotic plants. Facing the westerly rains, Muncaster Castle at the foot of Eskdale provides a wonderful show of rhododendrons and azaleas; it also has a 300 year old heronry, flamingos and exotic animals, but it has lost its red deer. Its 300 acres include big-leafed *Rhododendron sinogrande* and *macabeanum*, great scarlet *arboreum*, purple-blotched white *falconeri*, and the 'Muncaster hybrids'.

Lowther, near Penrith (730 acres), has red deer, but now has expanded its collection, with 130 acres of open safari zoo, to include Japanese (Formosan) sika from Pickering in Yorkshire and fallow deer from Woburn; greylag and Canadian geese, and black Australian swans, are some of its variety of waterfowl. In the same trend, Holker Park added red deer and sika to its menil fallow deer, but stopped short of wild boar. Its 22 acre garden contains Britain's oldest Chilean monkey-puzzle pine, which was planted by Paxton and later re-erected after it had been blown down in a storm. Magnolias, cherries, rhododendrons and azaleas are followed here by roses and flowering trees and shrubs, like *Paulownia*, *Eucryphia*, *Embrothium* and *Davidea*. The purple seed-heads of *Magnolia sieboldii* in winter burst open to show orange seeds, and then they rival the autumn splendour of spindle trees. Buzzard, shelduck and woodcock nest at times in the park, while herons nest in Old Park Wood nearby.

Levens, south of Kendal, is divided into two by the A6. On the east of the road are a deer park and an oak avenue, and on the west topiary gardens of mutilated box and yew, like giant chessmen, and a botanical menagerie, sheltered by a close-clipped beech hedge for the benefit of small birds in winter. Near Pelter Bridge by the Ambleside–Rydal road, the Lord's Oak marked the spot where the lord of the manor of Rydal Park received his rents. Even in winter magnolias make a grand show with their colourful seeds in gardens like those of Barrow House at Borrowdale, and Holker Hall with its *M. sieboldii.* Other notable gardens include Hutton John at Penrith; Hazelwood, where great New Zealand cypresses shelter a badgers' earth; Briery Close; and White Crags (Westmorland). Exotic conifers marked the old home of Christopher North in Elleray Woods.

The river path through Yewdale provides wood warbler, dipper, sandpiper, pied flycatcher, tree creeper and green woodpecker, and more juniper than yew on the way to Little Langdale or Low Oxen Fell. Roe have reached here also. Derwent Bank at Portinscale, gateway to the Newlands Valley, is the starting-point for many a nature walk; one may see cormorants flying up Derwentwater, watch goldeneye and mergansers diving in the lake, or walk down to Lingholme, where herons sometimes nest, woodcock call, and the woods echo with chaffinch and jay. In April when the dales are sunny, the surrounding mountains are still covered with snow. May brings sedge warblers, passing corncrakes, blackcaps, garden warblers, and goldcrests singing in the topmost larches. One may pass by Bassenthwaite and the brown shoulder of Grisedale Pike and make the long climb up the Whinlatter Pass, where chaffinches inhabit the dark pine woods. Finally, beside the Lorton fells, one may follow the rushing waters of Whit Beck to Cockermouth, where the sea trout come up on the spates. Mayfly do not hatch up here until well into June, but trout rise in the warmer weather and, with partridge and orange as a lure, one has every chance of a creel-full for supper.

The glacier that moved down Dunnerdale from the head of Wrynose left many signs after it passed between Grey Friar and Crinkle Crags, when it was joined by ice from the west. You can walk the bed of the Duddon glacier from Hall Dunnerdale to Cockley Beck, 700ft high beyond Dalehead, the junction of Hardnott and Wrynose passes, beyond Seathwaite. Mosedale probably marks the bed of an old lake, formed when the ice melted. Old copper-ore shafts show the way from Three Shire Stone to the Crinkles, and one's boots may still be stained red. From Cockley Beck with favourable weather it is only an hour to Eskdale Steeple, 2 hours to Dow Crag and 2½ hours to Bowfell, Scafell or Pavey Ark.

Wordsworth praised the Duddon in more than thirty sonnets hardly read today. Anyone who can walk just over 20 miles can go from Duddon Bridge to Ambleside through Cockley Beck and Wrynose, where one is on the Roman road from Ravenglass. Or at Ulpha one can turn up Crosby Gill for Devoke Water, where greylags sometimes breed.

Apart from the coastal New Red Sandstone on either side of the estuary where large flocks of teal and pintail gather in winter, and the Silurian rock on its south-east side, most of Dunnerdale consists of the Borrowdale Volcanic series. The coast was shaped by Scottish glaciers moving south across the Solway Firth, not by the Lakeland glaciers that carved out the dales, and so there are few dales like Duddon and Eskdale giving broad views down to the sea. Fells that once sloped to the western sea were sliced away, and the sand, clay and gravel left by the melting ice blocked the Rivers Ehen, Irt and Esk, and the Annaside and Whicham becks, and turned them along the coast before they could break through.

Mention should be made of the lowland 'Mosses', such as Scaleby Moss in the Irthing Valley with its Labrador tea-plants, Carlatton and Cumwhitton Mosses in the Lower Eden Valley,

Cliburn further up, Stainmore near Brough, Meathop, and the mosses and marshes along the Solway Firth from Bowness and Kirkbride to Newton and Skinburness, where marsh fritillary butterflies and marsh mallows flourish. Rusland Moss, Leighton Moss, Holker Moss and Glasson Moss are major insect haunts, especially for moths.

Page 125 (*above*) A small pearl-bordered fritillary butterfly, which lays on dog violets beside limestone woods, feeding from a thistle; (*below*) an ant-hill of pine needles made by the southern wood-ant in Arnside Park

Page 126 (*left*) A striped hawkmoth, one of the rarer migratory visitors to Lakeland from the continent; (*below*) feathery antennae mark this emperor from the larger empress moth, found in daylight on fell and heath

CHAPTER EIGHT

Rivers

MANY LAKELAND RIVERS have a similar character. Confined by rock and boulder and strengthened by many tributaries, they riot in winter spate and loiter in summer on their way from mountain to sea.

The nutriments brought down by a river to its estuary are spread by the incoming tide, fertilising the coastal zone, transforming channels and shorelines. Sand beds also retain useful organic matter from the falling tides, and this feeds and encourages a micro-fauna that supports estuarine shoals of sprats and flounders, immigrant eels, twaite shad, salmon and sea trout, among other estuarine animals evolved for life in a constantly changing environment; Man's plans for the Morecambe Bay and Solway barrages would make a more permanent change.

Most Lakeland rivers are clean, thanks largely to salmon and coarse-fish anglers, who joined forces to resist pollution long before conservation became fashionable. The rivers support twenty different fishes and, with other waters, 80 per cent of British stoneflies, 66 per cent of mayflies including *Protonemura montana* as a new British species, and 56 per cent of British caddisflies. Barbel, bleak and bream are missing, grayling are confined to the Eden and crayfish (crustaceans) are rare because of the low calcium content. A few white-clawed crayfish have been found in Westmorland streams running into Windermere, in upper tributaries of the Eden, especially near Melkinthorpe as well as its Yorkshire border headquarters at Abbotside Common, and in some Cumberland streams.

Vast hatches of the dark olive dun *Baetis atrebatinus*, a northern anglers' 'fly', swarm on some Cumberland rivers early in
the trout season. Sometimes the March brown *Rithrogena
haarupi*, the iron blue or 'watchet' *B. pumilis*, and the large
dark olive hatch in equally large numbers. A small stream near
Coniston is the only British haunt of the caddis *Glossosoma inter-
media*, whose large case is rounded at the top and flat beneath.
The grannon sedge has not been recorded in Lakeland, but great
red sedge, Welshman's button and caperer are here.

Pearls

Often talked about but rarely found, the pearls from Lakeland's
long oval black river mussel, *Margaritifera margaritifera*, are found
in the soft water of fast clean mountain rivers with a low lime
content, notably the Irt. They are often darker than oyster pearls
and smaller, with a greeny-mauve lustre, but may be white,
pinkish, greenish or brown. Glass-bottomed drums are used by
pearlers searching the river beds for their host mussel, bulkier
when carrying a pearl. The mussels are opened and then boiled
to a mulch with water, when the pearl sinks to the bottom.
Most beds were worked out in the eighteenth century, but
during droughts in World War II pearls were obtained from the
Ehen at Cleator, as well as from Cocker and Ellen. Many are
only tiny seed-pearls, and I have seen 'slugs' attached to the
mother-of-pearl and of no commercial use.

'Fair as Irton pearls' is an old Cumbrian proverb, quoted by
Camden. In 1777 an agent engaged locals to collect sufficient
from the river for London dealers to pay £800 for them; but
there is no record of how long this took or whether pearls
already collected were included. Pearl beds existed at Frizington,
Salter and right up to Ennerdale Lake. In the period of un-
employment between the World Wars, several men fished for
them from Hazel Home and upwards in the Ehen. I was told
in Cockermouth that two brothers named Delaney filled two
canisters with small pearls and sold them to a Whitehaven

jeweller for £5. In very dry summers when the Ehen is only a trickle, small pearls have been found near the bridge at Wath Brow. A Cockermouth jeweller, D. Scott, once had a nice small pearl that was found a short distance from Ennerdale Lake. Larger specimens were obtained from the river between Frizington and Cleator Mill; a Manchester firm paid £4 for one, 'snow white, the size of a pea'.

The trematode fluke-worm, which enters the mantle of the mussel and sets up the irritation that causes the secretion of nacre, or mother-of-pearl, around it, lives as an adult in swans or diving tufted duck. Its eggs pass into the water, or hatch into free-swimming larvae that enter the water. Reaching the mussel bed, it may re-enter the shellfish to end its life entombed in a pearl, or be devoured by a duck and the life cycle repeated. Scoter and scaup, suggested as carriers in Professor W. J. Dakin's old manual *Pearls*, can transport the worms only as far as estuarine mussels, as they are seldom up rivers. The difference between Lakeland and North Wales (Conway) pearls is that the latter are mostly from the edible estuarine mussel, the former, like Scottish pearls, from river mussels.

The Eden

Salmon hold pride of place in Lakeland rivers, and anything less than trout or char is vermin to its anglers. Improving the natural environment of the river is a more effective way of increasing the number of fish than the traditional hatchery and its repeated restockings. Salmon are unhampered by the cold, and only cease running when a river becomes too slow.

In dry springs and early summers, Morecambe Bay and the Solway are full of salmon waiting for a spate to urge them up the rivers, for the biggest salmon come up after heavy rainfall. The Eden is England's earliest salmon river, though its neighbour Esk is a late one. On early-closing days in Carlisle when the salmon are running up river in season, every sportsman is fishing this other Eden, with a golden sprat in spring or a Jock Scott in

summer, from Charlie's Neck at the foot of the Caldew tributary, past Paddie's Nose opposite the town bridge, to the Long
Pool just below Johnny Bulldog's Lane. As many as 150 salmon
may be taken in spring, especially in weather that Cumbrians
describe as 'a queer nice day'.

Spring finds teams of anglers 'skellie-fuddling' on the Eden's
tributary, the Irthing, at Newby Bridge, which means destroy-
ing the 'vermin' chub, locally called skellies, to make room for
more salmon and trout. The Eden is most familiar to visitors
from Eden Bridge on the main road to Scotland up river to New
Bridge, or down among the wild geese in its 4 miles of estuary
at Rockliffe, but it looks its best in the deep gorge at Wetheral,
a green mile of birds and plants. On the path below the church,
a splendid spot in spring and when autumn lingers into early
December in the shelter of Corby Castle woods, one may watch
late salmon still leaping under the viaduct at the end of the year.
Here, already paired, the dippers sing; and along the river path,
where trees hang green with polypody and grey with lichen
throughout winter, the greenhouse smell of spray-sodden moss
lies everywhere. The boat pool here is reputed to be one of the
best salmon pools in England.

The Eden was too deep and fast to freeze during the fierce
frost of December 1951, unlike the tarns, which lost all their
wild swans, grebe and coot to the deeper waters of Windermere
and other lakes, but its steep wooded valley became a frost trap.

There is a greener beauty in parts of the Eden Valley than
round the tourists' lakes. Few places equal the great Beech
Walk, a private greensward with trees and hundreds of daffodils, which runs for about a mile between rocks and river. The
monks of Wetheral's twelfth-century Benedictine priory made
the long narrow islands, still to be seen in the river, to guide
migrating salmon into their ancient coops, which serve now as
nesting places for dippers. Salmon-coops were also built at
Warwick Hall, not far away. Sir Walter Scott visited and praised
the beautiful landscape gardening at Corby Castle. Another
lovely stretch runs through the woods at Udford, beyond Pen-

rith, to Edenhall in the upper valley; but perhaps second to Wetheral is the country about Armathwaite watermill, especially in autumn.

Many salmon spawn in the Irthing, the Gelt and lower Eden. Out of every 1,000 salmon eggs laid in the winter spawning-beds up the Eamont, 50 are lost there to greedy parr, brown trout and grayling as spates wash them out; 900 reaching parr stage are eaten by herons, goosanders, cormorants, kingfishers, otters or even black-headed gulls from moorland gulleries; 49 more, migrating seawards as smolts, are eaten by Solway seals, or porpoises, cod and other predators before they reach the Irish Channel; and just one hefty grilse may survive the Greenland salmon-netters, the estuarine pollution, and poaching at home to spawn again in the tributary of its birth.

The source of the Eden 70 miles from Carlisle on Abbotside Common, intersecting Mallerstang Common in a bleak corner of the Pennines between Kirkby Stephen and Hawes is ignored by most salmon, which either turn up the Irthing, or vault Armathwaite weir, then, scorning Ullswater, travel up the Eamont. Before weirs were built, they entered the Caldew and the Petterill at Carlisle. When the salmon arrive, the fells have lost their summer tameness, feeding the river at Kirkby Stephen with dark and brimful becks that leap over many little water-falls absent from the summer scene. Except in very rainy autumns when the river tops its dams, few salmon ascend above the Eamont junction near Ullswater. The theory that Eden as well as Esk salmon came up the Scottish side of the Solway was exploded when the Corby catch more than doubled in the year following the removal of English stake-nets. Eden's salmon season is 15 January to 14 October.

Dace inhabit only the lower reaches, and pike up to 9lb live in the Irthing. The upper reaches belong to trout, and the gray-ling is destroyed as vermin. It is not a native fish but was intro-duced back in 1860. Chub, which also occur at Wetheral, are in the tributary Eamont, and the Eden, at Penrith. There are roach in the river, but few perch, which are more often lake fish.

Flounders ascend among the coarse fish at Rickerby Rocks. The Eden is also a sea-trout river, though not as good as the border Esk. These migratory forms of brown trout start to run in May and average 1½lb. Larger sea trout visit the Scottish side of Solway.

In addition to the migrating salmon that come through the Solway Firth from Greenland, or the Faroes, the seasonal life of the Eden includes the wild geese down at the estuary, the black-headed gulls that nest along Solway and with fishing goosanders come to Edenhall and Armathwaite weir, the herons that nest in the high wood above Corby Castle and at Dolphenby in the upper valley, and the cormorants that fish there and perch in the trees to roost in winter.

Hemmed in by high mountains, the Eden Valley is character-ised by its soft red sandstone, and in spate is often deep red. American monkey-musk and Himalayan balsam share its banks. Since 1920 at Ormside, oystercatchers have nested up its pebbly sides and in fields to Mallerstang. Sandpiper, dipper, grey wag-tail and occasionally mute swan and goosander also breed. Goosanders fish regularly within sight of spring salmon-anglers in haunts of buzzard and green woodpecker at Armathwaite. Willows tend to colonise the sandy and gravelly salmon-spawning beds in the upper reaches, to the railway bridge at Musgrave Road, Temple Sowerby. Shortly after daybreak one March morning I visited Whin's Tarn in the fells above Eden-hall heronry to watch a drake goosander and two whooper swans. This was one of the best winter waterfowl haunts then in the upper valley, with smew, shelduck, Bewick's swans, garganey and larger flocks of goosanders among its usual visitors, but it declined later.

The A66 in the Eden Valley is an approach to Cliburn Moss, near Temple Sowerby, a haunt of moths like the great mountain carpet (though not mountainous) and the goldenrod brindle, as well as of plants like bog-whortleberry.

The Esk

A 31lb sea trout caught in a Solway stake-net in 1904 was probably from the Border Esk, now classed as an English river, which starts as a brown-trout river in Dumfriesshire, but becomes primarily a sea-trout and salmon river from Langholm to the Solway. Sea trout and herling run up in quantity from June to August, salmon in spring and October. It is English geographically for 6 miles from Longtown to the Solway, where, late on December afternoons, thousands of golden plover race overhead, clouds of lapwings flutter past, and goldeneyes fly noisily in the gathering gloom, led by a black-and-white drake. Wigeon, mallard and curlew fill the foggy marsh, and snow buntings move along the saltings. When fowlers have been too active, many of the geese move to the Scottish side, and at one time one could only approach them with a black dog, because the Rockcliffe shepherd they trusted used one. The Esk's tributary, the Liddel, along the Scottish border, is a noted trout stream.

The Derwent

Flowing from the north side of Scafell through Borrowdale, Derwentwater and Bassenthwaite to Workington, the Derwent has salmon and trout throughout most of its length, yielding from 400 to 900 salmon according to the dryness or wetness of the season, and in 1872 a 57 pounder, though the average is $6\frac{1}{2}$lb. It has no grayling. Its rapid 35 miles flow drains 270sq miles—the waters of nearly 100 miles of streams, six large lakes and thirty small tarns.

It is a late river, with few salmon before September.

Over 700 sea trout were taken from the Derwent and its tributary Cocker in 1962, including as many as 350 in spectacular August spates and over 200 in October. Sea trout migrate up western rivers like the Derwent from July onwards, averaging $1\frac{1}{2}$ to 2lb. Big 8lb fish may come earlier, but they are less interested in bait or fly. Its spring salmon find a summer retreat in Bassenthwaite and Crummock. The 6 mile tributary, the Greta, as clear as a southern chalk stream in dry weather because of its glacial origin, and only 15 to 25yd wide, has one of the biggest salmon runs for any British river of similar size: salmon ascend it to spawn in the head streams of Thirlmere. It is far less attractive to sea trout and, owing to lack of weed, to brown trout.

Scale Force, Lakeland's highest waterfall at 125ft, is on Scale Beck, and feeds Crummock in the Cocker watershed. The next highest, Barrow Cascade, 108ft, is on Barrow Beck, which enters south-east Derwentwater. These are the only two Lakeland falls over 100ft, though there are half-a-dozen over 50ft. Many are rich haunts of ferns—for instance, Eskdale's Dalgarth Falls. Only sea trout from Moricambe Bay normally enter the Wampool at Kirkbride and the Waver at Abbey Town, and there are some flounders.

Other River Valleys

The Duddon, 25 miles long from Wrymose to its sandy estuary, is a good sea-trout river, with some salmon; but Seathwaite dam stops fish from ascending Tarn Beck. Trout and some char live in the tarn; but apart from a few ring-ouzels and common sandpipers, it has few birds, compared with Dunnerdale fells above Ulpha Bridge. This secluded valley lies in the north-west corner of the Furness fells, set apart from the rest of Lancashire, and nowhere else in the county in such a small compass is there such variety of scenery. It is too remote for trains and lacks the tripper-trade of Hawkshead; its few villages seem built into it in the same way as the naked rocks above. Stone bridges straddle the rocky stream where grey wagtails, sandpipers, dippers and mallard breed, where butterwort, marsh St John's wort and *Viola tricolor saxatilis* flower. Globe flower may also be seen up the Black Beck from its estuary.

It does not need Turner's exaggerated dawns and flaming

sunsets to enhance the view whenever one looks down the long valley rimmed by rough and rugged fells, its green fields stitched with dark stone walls. The grass always grows green, since *Agrostis* and *Fescue* have replaced the hard grey-blue *Mollinia* and *Nardus* grasses of the fells. Nature here shows her energy with unrestful angles and jagged skylines. This is not the soft peaceful scene of the Leven below Windermere, but landscape suited to storm and wind.

The rivers flowing into Morecambe Bay show a marked difference between the soft water coming off the millstone grit to the west—Leven and Crake—and the hard water off the limestone to the east—Kent, Keer, Bela, Winster and Gilpin. The Leven flows from Essdale Beck via Grasmere, and, leaving Rydal Water under the name Rothay, then joined by the Brathay from Elterwater, it drains Windermere and 202sq miles round about. In 1968 303 salmon were caught by its nets and rods, and 2,466 over 4lb were counted at the mechanical recorder at Haverthwaite in 1966. In 1965 2,133 sea trout were caught and 1,413 over 4lb recorded at Haverthwaite in 1966. Below Newby Bridge, pike and perch prey upon its trout and goldeneye dive here in winter. Even down at Low Wood Bridge many aquatic insects breed in the river, especially large olive and blue-winged olive mayflies, the stonefly *Amphinemura sulcicollis* and the caddis *Hydropsyche instabilis*. Its estuary supports flocks of wildfowl and waders at Park Bay, Holker and Sandgate near Flookburgh, especially concentrated at high tide and its ebb.

Mergansers breed on Bigland Tarn. The valley of the Crake takes salmon and sea trout to Coniston Water through haunts of grasshopper-warblers, otters and beds of flag iris. The Crake is occasionally mild enough for a wintering sandpiper or a greenshank, and its kingfishers survived the severe winter of 1962–3. The neighbouring Rusland Valley, with Grizedale at its head, is one of Lakeland's chief haunts of royal and rigid buckler ferns as well as of nightjars, and of roe and red deer. The Moss here is a national nature-reserve rich in moths. Its heronry is now near Haverthwaite. Oxen Park in the Crake

Valley supports nuthatch and kingfisher. Carp, roach, perch, eels and gudgeon have been introduced into the 1½ mile Ulverston Canal at the estuary. The River Kent, whose source lies near the peregrines' eyrie up the Kentmere Valley, is a trout river popular with both anglers and herons. It has no grayling. Frothing over Sedgwick Falls, a barrier to salmon but a haunt of dippers, it hurries below a hanging wood chockful of anemones and sweet violets in April, and curves through moss-hung limestone into the last of Kendal's former fifteen Elizabethan deer-parks. The stone bridge carrying the A5 crosses it near Levens Hall, and it finally reaches the sea below Arnside. The Kent is tidal to Underbarrow. In 1968 760 salmon were caught by its nets and rods and 493 sea trout in 1966. A few sparling spawn in its lower reaches, as they do in the Leven.

Sand martins burrow in the banks high up in Levens Park, where fallow deer have lived since the sixteenth century: there are now nearly fifty of the dark Scandinavian race which turn black in summer. The avenue of ancient oaks and the lovely river gorge rally conservationists to the Park's defence whenever it is threatened by planners. Thriving, though destructive to the trees, is a herd of black-faced black-necked Schwarzhal goats and their tribe of snow-white kids. The billies' great scimitar horns have given the manorial crest to the Bagot family, who introduced them here in 1962 from the ancestral Blithfield Park in Staffordshire. This Rhone Valley breed was named Bagot goat after Richard II had presented some to ancestors of the present Bagots. Enclosed by de Redeman in 1360, the park is on Saxton's map of 1576. The deer's traditional Scandinavian origin is connected with James I's marriage to Anne of Denmark, but black fallow were living at Windsor in 1465. More likely they are descended from the old dun deer of Norman and Roman hunting stock, which preceded the spotted fallow, introduced to fatten in parks for venison.

Flounders ascend from Arnside, and twaite shad and spawning sparling enter the Kent and Leven estuaries. In 25 miles through rock pools and shingle from the Kent's source 5 miles north-east of Windermere, wild duck are seldom absent. Winter flocks of 200 mallard are near Milnthorpe. Its tributary, the Gilpin, flows down the lovely broad Lyth Valley, famous for spring damson blossom (the Westmorland Prune) beside the A5074, from about 25 March to 12 May. This is a later strain than Cheshire and Shropshire damsons. About 700 trees grow on Draw Well farm, their success due to the limestone. In August and September the fruit attracts hawfinches and in spring bees. Scarlet heads of burnet mark the riverside meadows. Further up the valley, opposite Underbarrow, up to sixty canary-like siskins roam the woods at Crossthwaite in winter.

West of it lies the Winster Valley, falling gently from the limestone slopes of Brant Fell, 14 miles away near Bowness, to enter Morecambe Bay by Meathop's wild goose marshes 5 miles north of Grange. Rising and falling quickly without a lake to steady it, apart from Helton Tarn, the Winster receives more sea trout than salmon. The valley's limestone attracts flora that bring butterflies—dark green and high brown fritillaries, pearl-bordered and small pearl-bordered fritillaries, grayling, holly blue, a former colony of the small blue (it has isolated colonies on the sandstone railway cuttings of the Eden Valley), dingy skippers, brown argus and large heaths. Among its many moths are the rare barred tooth-striped moth, and the galium carpet moth probably at its southernmost point. There are clouded magpies and Portland daggers, blossom underwings and white-marked moths, while the butterbur moth ranges from here along the Leven Valley to Newby Bridge. Indeed, from Cartmel Fell to Eggerslack Wood above Grange a rich variety of *Lepidoptera* attracts attention on the hills above the Winster Valley. Common blues, small heaths and coppers flicker in summer sunshine, while wall browns and meadow browns are among the grassland and small pearl-bordered fritillaries abundant among the violets in June.

Winster Valley's wet mossy pastures grow grass-of-parnassus and marsh violet, its soft green fellside tiny leeks (the sand leek grows in the banks of Lake Windermere) and the lesser clubmoss

Selaginella. Oak, ash, birch and whitebeam provide pheasant coverts where the western scarp of Scout Scar plunges down from Whitbarrow into the valley.

It is an incomplete angler who finds only fish as he worms his way upstream or flails the water with a fly. The naturalist-angler sees spotted yellow balsam, 'touch-me-not', in the banks by Rydal, Ambleside and Bowness streams, water lobelia in Brathay and Rothay, viviparous fescue grass at Aira Beck, marsh St John's wort in the Duddon Valley, lesser wintergreen and filmy ferns at Stock Gill Force, and American monkey-musk and New Zealand willowherb spreading along most of the rivers.

Brown rats and water voles are often confused by countrymen as well as townsmen. With water shrews they inhabit the lower valleys. Alien mink spread from fur-farms into Ennerdale and wandered over the southern border from Wyresdale in north Lancashire, to be traced by fish-scales in their droppings. Two were caught in Cumberland in 1964. Otters, once widespread from Grasmere to the Eden, declined in the 1950s and 1960s. More often on the bank than in the water, they crossed fells, being trailed 10 miles in snow from one watershed to another. One bolted from a cairn at over 2,000ft. Another lived thirteen years beneath an old Cumbrian watermill, where its friends paraffined and blocked the holt against the Hunt.

Otters suffer persecution and cubbing from February on, and their survival is not so certain as the badger's.

Birds

The angler's interest in birds, like his interest in animals, should go further than seeking the jay's blue wing for his Jock Scott fly or spotting the flashy kingfisher by his pool. Though Ravenglass's mergansers were first recorded in error as goosanders, the latter's post World War II colonisation has been mainly along the rivers, and the former's, more successfully, on lakes. After beginning their colonisation of England by breeding in Upper Coquetdale in 1941, goosanders spread from North Tynedale into Lakeland, nesting at Bewcastle Beck on the border in the 1940s, in 1950 at the River Lyne and near Brampton, and later in the Eden Valley near Warwick Hall and at Langwathby. Up to eight at a time fish the middle Eden at Armathwaite, and elsewhere; but flocks of up to thirty or more may be seen on lakes like Hawes Water in winter. Though the red-breasted merganser has colonised mostly lakes and tarns, some ten pairs nest in the Esk Valley above Ravenglass.

Oystercatchers have been nesting 30 miles up the Eden for over forty years, even in fields 200yd from the river. Ringed plovers nest beside the lower tributaries and redshanks up to 2,000ft, laying in May. Moorhens are as much river birds as kingfishers and sandpipers. American pectoral sandpipers were greeted with gunshot at Edenhall in 1888 and at Levens Park in 1917, as was a squacco heron by the river at Kirkoswald in July 1845. Such an inhospitable reception was spared a golden oriole in Troutbeck Valley in the influx of August 1932, and subsequent visitors, treated with respect, nested in Grizedale Forest in 1958-9. The orange-breastbanded British subspecies of the dipper was first distinguished at Penrith in 1801. Herons ringed in Norway have ended their days at Ulverston and Satterthwaite, and one from Sweden died at Barrow.

Flooded fields attract winter herds of whoopers and wildfowl, as do the winter wheat and old potatoes by the A66 in the Eden Valley near Kirkby Thore. Mallard and teal flock to the river near Appleby. In the spring of 1967 when salmon disease was prevalent, goosanders at Armathwaite, among numerous mallard and wigeon, and black-headed gulls, were feeding on dead salmon covered with the subsequent fungus. Diseased fish were noticed there in 1972 also. The relation between birds and the diseases of fish is significant, for mergansers transport fish parasites, fish-eating gulls transmit British fluke-worms, and blackspot disease in fish is carried by herons and bitterns. One effect of the recent epidemic of salmon (and trout) disease was fewer but larger trout in the Eden at Armathwaite in 1972.

Becks

The becks that feed the rivers are journey's end for sea
trout and salmon. Brown trout and bullhead are the only fish
in the fast stony upper Tees becks on the boggy Moor House
reserve of eastern Westmorland, but there are ten stoneflies, eight
mayflies and various midges, black fly, caddis-creepers, water-
beetle larvae and freshwater shrimps for them to feed on, as well
as nematode round or thread worms to parasitise them. Here
linger shrubby cinquefoil, often trampled by trout anglers lower
down the Tees, and yellow marsh saxifrage on Meldon Fell
(2,200ft) and West Netherheath. Trout grow more slowly and
are smaller here than in the lakes, especially where the calcium
content is low. They bury themselves in the gravel when the
becks freeze. In many becks minnows compete with trout for
such food as the nymphs of aquatic 'flies' and filamentous algae
when they are spawning in the shallow gravels. Dark beck trout
average 3–4lb. American rainbow trout (correctly called steelhead in the USA) have been introduced to the Kent and the
Eden but seldom spawn. The Cumberland River Authority has
a salmon-hatchery and a trout-hatchery at the Castle fisheries,
Cockermouth. *Myosotis brevifolia* grows frequently beside the
becks.

Salmon journeying to and from the Faroes or the Greenland
Sea are splendid navigators, but the larval eel drifts with the Gulf
Stream, then switches its behaviour to wriggle upstream against
the flow. The eel's breeding pattern is also opposite to that of
the salmon. The female, after a dozen years, and the male, after
about nine, return downstream with the flow, then swim against
the Gulf Stream to breed in the depths of the Sargasso Sea, where
their journey originated. Eels' river diet is far less damaging to
trout eggs than used to be assumed. Sea and river lampreys
molest the fish but the non-parasitic brook lamprey does not.

Walking beside rivers is not enough; one must camp by them,
in all seasons, to study them properly, for most of their fauna is
nocturnal.

CHAPTER NINE

The Cumbrian Coast

WHEN THE ARNSIDE link road is built to Whitehaven, it will open
a door to 70 miles of Lakeland coast. The 866sq miles of National
Park at present excludes south Cark and the Cartmel Peninsula,
the seabird citadel at St Bees Head, the migration watch at Grune
Point and England's greatest wildfowl haunt along the Solway
Firth, but these areas have always attracted Lake District naturalists. Walney and Ravenglass are of national importance, and
Duddon's golden sands, the flower-decked bird cliffs at St Bees,
the autumn tints among the coppiced woods of Furness, and the
view down Eskdale to the sea are scenes of great beauty. 'Over
the sands', the mild green and grey land round the north end of
Morecambe Bay, was as much part of Lancashire until the
boundary changes as Coniston and Furness, though there was a
bit of Westmorland at Arnside. Lakeland's naturalists also include
the bird-rich reedbeds of Leighton Hall Moss and the limestone
plant-rarities of Silverdale and Arnside, even Hutton Roof, in
their terrain. Twenty-four species of wader favour the shores of
Morecambe Bay. Over 1,800 shelduck have been counted at
Duddon Hawes in winter.

One June the Merseyside Naturalists' Association's north-
western shelduck breeding census counted 849 adults with 180
young between North Walney and the Duddon and 410 in the
Kent estuary; and in 1968 it noted 1,560 adults in north Morecambe Bay. Many flights may be seen migrating inland over the
Keer estuary at dusk early in July, to moult off Heligoland
Bight.

Let us begin with the Kent estuary, and look down from the elevated limestone rock of Arnside Point, from which, sheltered by the thick wood of yews in Arnside Park, we may watch the tidal bore flooding the mudbanks below Grange and disturbing its winter flock of mallard, a scene we shall lose if the Morecambe Bay barrage is erected. Morecambe Bay is Britain's leading haunt of wader flocks with a count of 252,443 in December.

The 400 flooded acres of reed and iris at Leighton Hall Moss, the former valley of Leighton Beck below Silverdale railway-station bridge and our miniature Hickling Broad is the result of failing drainage after World War I and opposition to farmers who wished to drain it. This is a major breeding ground of the bittern in Britain, from February to June, with nine breeding pairs. Osprey and marsh harrier are regular birds-of-passage in May and often autumn; rarer visitors have ranged from the big Caspian tern to the little bearded tit which summered here in 1972. All these birds may easily be observed—just a field's distance from the Yealand Storrs road, or down the causeway bisecting the reed where up to thirty pairs of reed warblers nest, and from a public footpath to the back of the castellated mansion of Leighton Hall and Yealand village. Occasional red deer and red squirrel hide in the woods nearby, and northern marsh orchid flowers at the Moss: rich in dragonflies, it has 16 species of butter-fly and 276 moths.

Long before Leighton Moss became a Royal Society for the Protection of Birds reserve, I recorded its bitterns nesting (back in 1946) and feeding on its eels, roach and frogs. Birds now nest on both sides of the causeway and sometimes stand displaying on it—or, like the otters here, stand on the winter ice on Storrs Moss pool. One sometimes booms in Bassenthwaite reeds; the male's deep boom, like that of a Mersey ferry, can sometimes be heard, with favourable wind, on Silverdale station. On moonlit March nights I have left the Barrow train at Silverdale to walk down lane and causeway, and heard them while woodcock flew roding overhead, snipe drummed, water rails squealed like pigs, lapwings buzzed their wingtips in territory flight and sometimes

Page 143 (right) Autumn ladies'
tresses orchid; the north
Lancashire and Westmorland
limestone is its northernmost
British haunt;
(below) moss-leaved saxifrage, a
May–June alpine on basic rock

Page 144 (left) Purple mountain saxifrage, a spring alpine growing in basic soil in the fast-drained face of lichened rock; (below) starry saxifrage overlooking Levers Water on Coniston Old Man, showing typical rosettes of broad leaves

the last of the Kent estuary greylags flew over, gaggling as stridently as the farmyard geese that called in reply.

Seventy nesting species, including up to fifteen pairs of grass-hopper warblers, live mainly on the Moss, including the nor-thernmost colony of reed warblers, the spotted crake (once), seven kinds of duck (mallard, teal, pochard, shoveler, tufted duck, wigeon [occasionally] and garganey), redshank, marsh and willow tits, and in nearby woods long-eared owls, woodcock, hawfinches (Woodwell), green woodpeckers, buzzards and others. The water here is probably too shallow for great crested grebes to colonise, but is visited by the smaller black-necked and Slavonian grebes.

Its noisy black-headed gullery is replaced in autumn by a starl-ing roost, raided by sparrowhawk and occasional peregrine. Over 160 types of birds have been recorded here, numbers going up to 1,500 winter mallard, 450 coot, 175 waxwings (in Grizedale Wood, October 1965), 300 wigeon, 100 teal, 100 shoveler and 50 pintail, with gadwall up-ending in the shallows. Black tern are commoner in spring than in autumn, when spotted redshanks and little gulls arrive. Rarities have included marsh sandpiper, goshawk, purple heron, goosander and spoonbill. Whooper and Bewick swans are regular winter visitors, and sometimes bearded tits are seen.

I once took home a whooper swan after it had lingered for weeks on Leighton Moss before dying of lead-shot poison, as my post-mortem of its liver revealed. A public notice at Leighton Moss reads: 'RSPB Bird-Reserve—Private'. But I have seen the sky criss-crossed with hundreds of wings rising to escape regular outbursts of gunfire from inside the sanctuary right and left of the causeway. Duck crumpled up in the air to tumble into Storrs Moss pool, and we watched a dog retrieve the corpses. Siberian Bewick swans, half a dozen of them, swam away from the disturbance. The curious anomaly of these regular shoots at a wild birds' sanctuary was due to a condition of the lease. *The New Wildfowler in the 1970's* listed it among 'National Wildfowl Refuges'.

I

Bittern and water rail nest also in the reeds of nearby Hawes Water, a small lake with few other birds, though occasionally visited by Leighton's ospreys and marsh harriers. This is a state reserve for its shell-marl deposits in which bird's-eye primrose and butterwort flower, at the lakeside end of its woodland path, with fragrant and dwarf purple orchids. Twayblade and early purple orchids grow along this path with deadly nightshade, and the lane is banked with sweet violets, and common and alder buckthorns. Bittern and osprey sometimes fly between here and Storr's Moss. In it grow fen sedge, bog rush, flat-stalked pondweed *friesii*, bladderwort and tussocks of horseshoe vetch.

Though dunlin and redshank nest occasionally on the shore at Silverdale and Arnside, the cutting of sea-washed turf has affected the wintering flock of greylag geese that comes here at times from Meathop to feed and, like sheep-grazing, reduced sea purslane, sea lavender and sea blite. Low limestone cliffs, bordering the saltmarsh of thrift, sea milkwort, sea lavender, meadow oat and mud rush, where the waders flock at the turn of the autumn tide from Arnside to Silverdale Cove, are cushioned with horseshoe vetch, wild wallflowers, baneberry, buckthorn, bloody cranes-bill, meadow dropwort, burnet rose, columbine, blue moor grass, wood and mountain melic grasses, small dwarf centaury, and occasionally Ceterach fern.

The sheep-grazed saltmarshes comprise creeping fescue and bent, with clumps of tall fescue in brackish parts, or of reed, rush or sedge and sea clubrush. At the higher levels are Gerard's mud rush, sea couch grass, sea and buckshorn plantains, sea pink, sea milkwort and sea spurry. Lower down grow sea poa and marsh samphire, while *Spartina anglica* grows at places like Cartmel. The sheep tend to eliminate sea purslane, sea lavender and sea blite. The extension of the saltmarsh attracted the greylags in the 1920s. Sea hard-grass, reputedly in its northernmost range on the Westmorland coast, was found on Cumberland's also, near Flimby. Geese also feed up Lunesdale, opposite Gressington.

The River Kent flows into the sea at Arnside; its south bank is approached from Milnthorpe, and its north bank via the A590 at

Levens, until the Arnside by-pass is built. Pinkfoot geese pass in autumn and spring, but the estuary feeds our southernmost wintering flock of 80–300 Icelandic greylags; 300 have been seen roosting on Meathop outer marsh as late as the end of March and feeding on the inner marsh below Lower Meathop Farm, as well as on Arnside Marsh. Milnthorpe Marsh, Sandgate and Arnside attract over 800 mallard and teal in winter. Many pie-bald shelduck making summer evening moult-migrations are a noticeable sight across the sands.

Wigeon and mallard winter off Grange, where there may be 500 dunlin, as well as sanderling, occasional curlew-sandpiper and 100 or more curlew. Pintail join the duck in November. I have seen spotted redshank and little stint at low tide at the end of the grey spur of Humphrey Head, where 10,000 oystercatchers sometimes come to roost. There may be blue-shouldered com-panies of greylags, or over 300 of the darker smaller pinkfeet in autumn and spring. Packs of wigeon and teal ride up on the winter tide, which flows less than 5 hours but ebbs about 8 hours. Spoonbill and avocet are rarer visitors. Summer brings the botanists to the only northern station of goldilocks aster, on Humphrey Head, along with decreasing rock samphire, western spiked speedwell, bloody cranesbill, hoary rock-rose, spotted cat's ear, milk vetch, Portland spurge and sea cottonweed. In 1959 *Spartina anglica* cordgrass appeared. Here also are the *crassifolius* variety of birdsfoot trefoil, angular shield fern and the *compactum* variety of crow garlic. Another interest is the beetle *Gonodera luperus*.

Behind the bulging gasometer below Meathop Lane, from Grange, and only 20ft up the limestone cliff of the old quarry overlooking the estuary below Limegarth Wood (a few hundred yards from the Arnside–Grange viaduct), the black wiry stems of the maidenhair fern are at their northernmost, apart from a spot above the Leven estuary at Greenodd. At night little roe steal out of Seattle Wood and Meathop Moss. Roaming sika stags from Bowland's Dale Head, lacking sufficient sika hinds produce fertile hybrids with closely related red hinds. Dark red helleborine, Norwegian cinquefoil and maidenhair grow at Meathop quarry.

Opposite Greystones Garage near Lindale on the road from Grange, where the Winster divided the former Lancashire from Westmorland, a field bridle-path choked with birch and bracken leads up over peat and heather and through a thicket of bog myrtle, pine and rowan to an old drying bog full of marsh andromeda, golden asphodel, cotton-grass and cranberries. This is the last northern haunt of the dark *philoxenus* variety of the large heath or marsh-ringlet butterfly, which has large eyespots on its hind wings. In its damper days this peat bog, now 4–5ft higher than the surrounding farmland, was turned into a nature reserve by the SPNR to conserve the butterfly. But the spread of birch, rhododendron, pine, heather and bracken into the bog as it has dried has endangered its insects and flowers and long-leaved sundew. It seems to have lost Massey's variety of silver-studded blue, which lingers across the estuary on Arnside Knott and up the Winster at Witherslack. Autumn still brings the purple-bordered gold moth, common on many Lakeland moors, and the Manchester treble bar, bordered grey, clouded buff, grass wave and small emerald breed on the reserve. I once met a lesser black-backed gull standing like a sentry, and flushed his mate from her nest—they were the only remaining members of a once flourishing gullery here and at Foulshaw.

Down Cartmel Peninsula, Flookburgh is a shrimping centre. Large flocks of knot, redshank and up to 20,000 dunlin are here in mid-winter. One may set out on a spring walk from Cartmel, across fields, through Lane Park Wood's blue-and-white thickets of bluebells and stitchworts, down a lane of cranesbills to the herd of the menil race of fallow deer in Holker Park, and finish up by sitting on the top of the Old Park Wood badger earth. This walk starts with long views of distant Morecambe Bay, and ends overlooking Plumpton Viaduct and Chapel Island in the Leven Estuary. The light creamy menil is the most attractive of the four races of fallow deer, dappled with white spots all the year, unlike the common kind. No black borders the white rump. The 200 acres of Holker Park have the largest herd of this race, though some are also found at Dallam Tower and often seen from the A6 near Milnthorpe. Their origin is obscure. (Formerly an obsolete term for all speckled forms of fallow—and the flea-bitten colour of spotted ponies—the word menil may have originated from an erroneous belief that the deer were imported from Manilla, or from the Arab village of Menil on the Tigris, once the haunt of Mesopotamian fallow deer.) Holker's herd is kept to about 130, which has been walled in the park for over 230 years without any change of blood. When alarmed, the herd bunches and gallops off, led by a wise old doe, rarely bothering to hide like the dark Scandinavian race in Levens Park. So minute is their range that only odd ones stray to Roudsea Wood, though roe visit the park from the Ludderburn side of Cartmel Fell, from Bigland and the Rusland Valley woods. One may see the park's herds of fallow and red deer from the railway train between Cark and Ulverston.

In late September or early October the rut begins, when the smaller herd links up. Holker Moss and nearby Roudsea Wood support about thirty-two roe, and about five young are born in a year. Red deer seldom came nearer than Bigland Tarn until a new woodland deer-park was established, with thirty red deer, mainly of the famous Warnham (Sussex) strain. Japanese sika deer have also been established in the park, but it was decided not to introduce wild boar, at least for the present.

Nightjars linger on the estate and Holker Moss is a notable haunt of moths, from fen wainscot and satin lutestring to small brindled beauty, satin, oak and lilac beauties, sharp-angled peacock and many more. Purple hairstreak butterflies and brim-stones inhabit the trees bordering Burn Barn Wood.

Holker Moss is a natural extension of the state nature reserve, Roudsea Wood, which has already been mentioned (p 76). Some 134 species of moth come to its lamp traps on July nights, in-cluding the lichen-feeding red-necked footman. Blue-bordered carpets, Merveille du Jour, large wainscot, swarms of orange underwing early in the year, double dart and many alder and ash-feeding moths live in this verdant refuge, as well as purple hairstreak butterflies and the large yellow sedge or caddis. Over fifty species of larger fungi mark September here. Grayling, dingy skipper and hedge brown butterflies range up the coast (as at Drigg) and the large heath flies on Solway Mosses (and also has a moorland form).

Winter goldeneye fly up to Newby Bridge, a few wigeon and mallard, even a February smew, to Rusland Pool, and a black-necked grebe and 30 goldeneye visited Greenodd one December; but most of the duck are down in the Leven estuary, where January brings 5,000–10,000 off Allithwaite—mallard, wigeon, teal, pintail, shoveler, mergansers, scaup (100 one winter) and shelduck. Greylag occasionally make a temporary roost on the outer sands. Backed by strong wind, the tide can rise 16ft over Flookburgh's sheep-grazed turf. Hundreds of curlew appear here, with 3,000 duck of five species. The ebbing estuary is black with waders—up to 15,000 redshank, and 20,000 dunlin, the most numerous, as well as sanderling, knot and hordes of oystercatchers. Scoter come into Plumpton Hall Bay, and Holker Park Bay sometimes has over 1,000 wigeon and other duck below Barker Scar. Here the botanist finds spring cinquefoil, rock samphire, squinancy wort, spiny rest-harrow, tutsan, knotted pearlwort, field gentian and autumn ladies' tresses. Further down the coast, Sandgate Bay below Cark has had 200 shoveler and 100 scaup with its teal and mallard, and, in hard winter weather here and at Meathop, flocks of up to 2,000 lapwings driven out of the northern hills. The recovery in the Leven estuary of a cormorant ringed on the Farne Islands showed the birds' cross-country dispersal.

Chapel Island in the Leven, like Piel Island off Rampside, is the high-tide roost in winter for up to 100 cormorants and packs of oystercatchers, while up to 150 scaup swim nearby. Over 30,000 oystercatchers feed out on Cartmel Wharf, and, until the severe winter of 1962–3 decimated the cockle beds, they took nearly a quarter of the young shellfish. The birds then resumed their old habit of feeding on earthworms in the fields; 200,000 or more have been estimated on Out Marsh, west of Humphrey

Head and West Plain Marsh (below Flookburgh), apart from birds at Arnside and Silverdale—20,000 gather at South Walney in frosty spells. Few remain to nest, most of them leaving for Scotland, Iceland, Scandinavia and the Faroes. Some 17,000 were destroyed, after long-term studies by the Lancashire Sea Fisheries' Committee, mainly by fly-netting at night between Grange and Ulverston, without appreciably affecting their population. The nets were 3,250yd long and netting was stopped after the capture of some other birds (later released), including razorbill, dunlin, redshank, knot, golden plover, cormorant, and one owl. The fishery officer reported the capture of a 'dotterel' but it was a ringed plover, under its old local nickname of 'ringed dotterel'.

Most coastal birds are natural predators upon littoral marine life. The poor quality of flounders in the Kent and Leven estuaries in 1971 was attributed by the Sea Fisheries' Committee biologist to the predation by oystercatchers upon the small bivalve *Macoma baltica*, an important part of flounders' food, as well as on mussels. Large winter flocks of redshanks have fouled beds of periwinkles with their droppings here. Even the rock pipit feeds on tiny periwinkle shells. Curlew here feed on *Macoma*, as well as 'hen-fish' and ragworms; redshanks on the almost amphibious *Hydrobia ulvae* (gastropod shellfish) and on the amphipod crustacean *Corophium volutator*; dunlin on *Hydrobia* and *Macoma*; knot on *Macoma*, and bar-tailed godwits on *Macoma*, cockles, hen-fish and *Hydrobia*. The latter little shellfish also attracts the shelduck, which sometimes number over 1,800 at Duddon Hawes.

Further down the coast, overlooking the estuary at Bardsea, I have been kept awake by the wild cries of curlews and piping oystercatchers. Up to 250 scaup have been seen in Bardsea Bay in December, and at Canal Foot below Ulverston wigeon flock in January with mallard, shelduck and great flocks of waders, including golden plover. Up to 5,000 knot have been counted on Roosebeck shore, and 450 wigeon, mallard and shelduck. North Morecambe Bay is Britain's major haunt of knot, with April flocks of 85,000.

Except at high tide, the long causeway from Rampside, where

Mertensia (the oyster-plant) grew, leads to Foulney Island. Five terns, including roseates and little terns, have bred on the island since the last century, but hordes of predatory gulls from Walney bird sanctuary seldom permit many first clutches or broods to survive. The red expanse of herb robert made a remarkable sight on the shingle around our hides when we first photographed the roseates and little terns. We counted 229 nests of arctic tern, 102 of common tern, and 13 of little tern. Eiders and Sandwich terns arrived later. By July 500 knots and 200 dunlin were on the sands and an arctic skua pursued the terns, and in August Rampside marsh had a wood sandpiper. Flocks of 1,000 dunlin come later, and a turnstone ringed by a friend on the Mersey was recovered here. Wigeon feed on *Zostera* here in winter, and there is meadow saxifrage, sea beet, sea campion, sea poppy, dovesfoot cranesbill and nine sorts of seaweed.

From Barrow to Vicarstown, where one sees and hears a bawling crowd of 45,000 lesser black-backed and herring gulls, Europe's biggest ground colony dominates the duneland sanctuary of South Walney Island. The lesser black-backed gull began nesting here in 1926. Flotillas of young eiders are escorted by ducks from some of the 300 pairs breeding. Nearly 200 drake eiders flock off Sheep Island in Piel Channel. The first eider's nest, discovered by the late F. Swarbrick off the lighthouse in 1949, still marks their southernmost colony on the west coast, though birds wander further south in winter.

Walney's unbroken curve of sand and shingle runs for 11 miles, and it is England's fourth largest island; 150 species of bird have been recorded there since Britain's first frigate petrel, now in Carlisle Museum, in 1890. Some 30 nesting species at the south end include 10–12 pairs of black-headed and 12 of great black-backed gulls, 50 pairs of oystercatcher, 30 pairs of ringed plover, 200 pairs of Sandwich tern and as many common, 150 arctics and 15 pairs of little tern. The little owl, sand martin, wren, stonechat and reed bunting also nest. Flocks of over 28,000 knot and 470 bar-tailed godwits have been counted here in midwinter. There are winter flocks of goldeneye, teal, wigeon and sea duck and waders in the southern bay, and Walney has also been visited by black guillemot, grey phalarope, purple sand-piper, and other waders at big tides, spoonbill, Cory's, sooty and Manx shearwaters, longtail duck, velvet scoter, the rarer grebes, marsh harrier, osprey, brent geese, skuas, melodious and yellow-browed warblers, black redstart and American white-throated sparrow. Shearwaters, skuas and divers are best with strong westerly winds. Merlin, short-eared owl and hoodie crow are among its winter visitors when big flocks of teal, wigeon, shel-duck and mallard rest in the bay. Turnstones often summer here.

Walney terns have had a chequered career. Originally the island was colonised from Drigg Point by common and Sand-wich terns, which nested like some gulls at the north end, but they were disturbed by the development of Vicarstown and moved to the shingle spit below the south end where grow sea-pinks, sea campion, horned poppy, seakale, viper's bugloss, silverweed and hound's tongue. Terns also nest at the north end where, at the time of writing, negotiations are proceeding for a reserve. At the south spit we photographed the birds from hides, as we did the nesting roseate, little and arctic terns. Persecution from the increasing gullery drove the roseates to the old ternery on Foulney, but wiser protection of the spit in recent years has brought them back with the Sandwich terns. Stints, spotted red-shanks and commoner waders crowd here and at Piel Island in frosty spells.

Yellow-striped natterjack toads survive here (and at Drigg, on Solway and formerly at Ulverston, Beck Heads Wood and Fen, and Murside Moss, north Lancashire). Common (not sand) lizards, palmated newts and sticklebacks breed, and there are hedgehogs, weasels, stoats, hares, rabbits, foxes, voles, long-tailed field mice and shrews, but I have not seen any moles. The wolf spider *Lycosa agricola* hunts the southern shingle, the long-legged household *Tegenaria atrica* is common in the gullery, and the little jumping spider *Euophrys frontalis* is there.

An occasional grey seal hauls out at Roa Island, bottle-nosed dolphins pass frequently, and killer whales and white-sided dolphins have been stranded. Chitons, limpets, winkles, dog whelk and *Tellina crassa* are among the seashore shells.

Seaweed was collected commercially on the west shore in 1971, and there is a rich marine flora in the north-west Walney channel. Walney's major botanical interest is the Lancashire cranesbill, *Geranium sanguineum lancastriense*, which is grown in gardens and was once considered a separate species; it is a pink and white form of the procumbent seaside form of bloody cranesbill. Both flourish in the roadside turf at Biggar Bank beyond thickets of burnet rose, and the two forms sometimes hybridise. Some still grows at the north end, together with marsh helleborine orchid and sea-bindweed. *Lancastriense* on rare occasions has appeared as a sport among coastal bloody cranesbills in Cheshire. England's southernmost *Mertensia* survives on the edge of the pebbly south-west dunes. Pyramid orchid and sea convolvulus, henbane, ploughman's spikenard, centaury, sea lavender, golden dock and dark mullein brighten the lighthouse dunes. We were surprised to see the spiked star of Bethlehem here, but seed may have drifted from the mainland. Tasselated grape hyacinth still grows by the bird-observatory cottage, as it does at Sandscale and Silloth.

The warm water of Barrow's large and little used Cavendish Dock became interesting when it attracted flocks of wigeon and diving duck, including a record count of about 1,000 pochard in November 1967. It became the moult-migration destination of mute swans from as far as Oxford; 15,000 young Indian grass-carp were introduced to feed on its choking pondweeds, in 1964.

Sandscale Haws, off Roanhead at the nearby Duddon estuary, is conserved for orchids such as the marsh, green-flowered and duneland helleborines, pyramid, northern and early marsh, bee and coral-root, and also has yellow birdsnest (*Monotropa*), blue fleabane, autumn felwort and field gentian, grass-of-parnassus, seaside centaury, yellow pansy and acrid lettuce. Little terns, the dragonfly *striolatum* and the sand dart moth are there. Up Dunner-dale, tracks lead from Foxfield station to the viaduct marsh in one direction and Angerton Marsh in the other. Flocks of mergansers fish for sprats and sand eels on the latter; October flights of greylags sometimes come down on their way to Arnside and flocks of waders move among the waves. Wader-counts have totted up 17,942. Mallard, teal, wigeon and shelduck flock here.

A green quilt of turf on the opposite shore marks Under-hill saltmarsh, and the South Cumberland fowlers' reserve at Hawes, visited by pintail, teal, wigeon, a few barnacle geese and waders. Flocks of greylags have been introduced to this 100 acre reserve of marsh and wood.

Up the coast at the Eskdale junction of Irt, Mite and Esk, is the famous duneland bird sanctuary on Drigg Point, known as Ravenglass because one formerly crossed the estuary from that fishing village. The approach now is from Drigg Shore Road (with a permit from the county land agent in Carlisle). Since the seventeenth century Britain's largest colony of black-headed gulls, it is now second to Needs Oar Point in Hampshire and has some 160 pairs of Sandwich terns, here since 1887, as well as a few arctic, common and little terns, oystercatchers, ringed plovers, shelduck, wheatears and, in low marram sandhills, mer-gansers, which in 1950 began their post-war colonisation of Lakeland in the Esk arm. In 1971 it had about 10,727 nests of black-headed gulls. Foxes by night and crows by day prey on eggs and chicks. The increasing herring and lesser black-backs from Walney would have colonised Drigg Point, too, had not their nests been destroyed. Shepherd's cress sprinkles these breezy dunes with tiny white flowers, and there are wild pansies, silver-weed, Canadian fleabane, sand sedge and interesting lichens. Common lizards thrive but its natterjacks suffer in dry springs. Nettle, ragwort and bracken flourish on the guano, as at Walney.

Curlew and lapwing nest on Drigg Common, and herons come to fish from Muncaster Castle heronry nearby. Here, up-river, sandpipers, tree pipits and snipe nest and there are wood-cock woods and blackcock fells. In winter 1,000 wigeon share the flooded Esk meadows with mallard and teal, and flocks of waders, scoter, wigeon, mallard and other duck frequent the estuary. Fishermen still drag their seine nets ashore by horse, and fish for dabs, plaice, crabs and the occasional lobster. Lumps of peat washed ashore by winter storms come from a submerged forest of birch, here and on Solway. As at Walney, you may see non-breeding dunlin and turnstone in summer, and the hedge-brown butterfly along the coast. In August 12,800 waders have been counted here.

A long winding lane from the Cumbrian village of Sandwith, with its corn buntings, or the long cliff paths from the mining village of Kells on the edge of Whitehaven, or St Bees to the south, lead one to the whitewashed lighthouse above the 365ft cliffs of St Bees. This viewpoint gives a splendid vista of the Irish Sea, with onshore west winds bringing gannets and occasionally shearwaters inshore among the gulls, or of the lobstermen setting their pots for crabs. Relays of auks and a chorus from some 50 kittiwakes below mark the seabird citadel. Fulmars glide across the cliff face and loud-voiced herring gulls try to dominate the scene. From the clifftop one sees 200–300 nesting guillemots and many razorbills, though barely half a dozen pairs of puffins. Black guillemots (two pairs) breed on the north and sometimes south heads. Lower down are black cormorants and jade-coloured shags on their nests. A few great black-backs and rock doves or feral pigeons, wrens, rock pipits, many starlings and jackdaws breed hereabouts, the season beginning at Tarn Flat quarry cliff ravenage. It is several years since peregrines nested, but choughs were here in 1955, and there are sometimes twite and stonechats in the gorse above Fleswick Bay.

These New Red Sandstone cliffs at St Bees have become a natural rock-garden for nitrophilous plants: sea pink and sea campion, bluebell and primrose, masses of bloody cranesbill, sheepsbit, tangled wood vetch, yellow patches of birdsfoot trefoil, umbels of alexanders, and scurvy grass according to season, flourish on the guano. The path dips down to Fleswick Bay, where at low tide one may view right beneath the precarious perches of the auks on the South Head, sift the pebbly beach for the rarer agates, search the rocks for sea spleenwort, rock sam-phire, or English stonecrop, set cod-lines, or in winter find purple sandpipers with the turnstones. Pock-marked with limpets' resting holes the low-tide rocks below the ledges have pools full of sea-anemones, corallines and other marine invertebrates.

Occasionally in winter whooper swans join the mutes and duck on colliery subsidence waters at Siddick and St Helens near Workington, or pinkfeet visit Allonby; and waterfowl visit Woodend Pool near the River Ehen and the A5086 at Egremont. But it is further north, at Silloth, where wildfowl and waders rather than scenic photographers make the Solway Firth a major attraction in autumn and winter. The Firth's legal boundary starts at Hodbarrow Point at Millom, and encompasses the whole Cumberland coast; but it is from Skinburness that one reaches its first main fall of migratory birds at Grune Point, where some sixty-six species of passerines and other migrants have been ringed. Barred and melodious warblers are among autumn species. Autumn waders are another attraction. Greylags and occasional barnacle geese come here and to Cardurnock across Moricambe Bay.

The Wampool and Waver estuaries, Wedholme floods and Oulton gravel-pits are worth visiting. Black-tailed godwits summer in the bay. Barnacles also come down near Bowness Common and I have seen them on Rockcliffe shore below Carlisle, though their main haunt is on the Scottish side. Wigeon, scaup, goldeneye and others feed on the *Zostera* at Calvo and Skinburness, and also on the Long Newton marshes and the Burgh shore, where common and arctic terns nest at intervals to Rockliffe. At Glasson Moss, a peat-cutting bog near Port Carlisle, a 140 acre state reserve shares with Oakmere in Cheshire the scarce little money-spider *Centromerus laevitarsis*. Marsh fritillaries are common. Bowness gravel-pits, and Calvo-Wedholme marsh and Moss by the B5307 are interesting.

The Solway is Britain's fifth largest wader haunt, with a count of 79,896 in the estuaries census (December 1970). It is the fourth largest haunt of knot, with flocks of 1,000-5,000. An American buff-breasted sandpiper visited Burgh as far back as 1876; black terns nesting in 1855, and dunlins since, have added to Solway's interest, as have little gull, little stint, curlew-sandpiper, curlew, and masses of golden plover flighting in winter down the nearby Esk. (Sark, not Esk, is the Scottish border.) Black-tailed godwits nested near Rockliffe in 1969, and there are black-headed gulleries at Scales Marsh (Faugh), above Kipford, near Rockliffe and Skinburness Marsh. Other visitors to Solway are pomerine and great skuas, red-necked and black-necked grebes, glossy ibis, night and purple squacco herons, great northern divers, Iceland, glaucous and Sabine's gulls, scaup and Iceland redshank.

From mid-September to mid-April, Solway's 75 species of wildfowl, waders and gulls bring birdwatchers from all over Britain. Of its five kinds of geese, pinkfeet outnumber all the rest put together, especially on the 1,600 acre Rockliffe marsh between Eden and Esk. In the 1970–1 estuaries counts, the south shore of Solway had Britain's biggest counts of pinkfeet (6,820), barnacle geese (3,432) and greylag (1,100), and of common gulls. The Spitzbergen barnacle geese are also claimed to be seen, with occasional Russian and Greenland whitefronts, and bean geese from Loch Ken. The late Colonel Hawker's famous punt-gun once struck terror into the Solway geese and duck, but we now prefer live pinkfeet to the sad-eyed corpses in the glass coffins of Carlisle Museum.

Around 1,000 wigeon winter at the Eden estuary, with a few teal, goldeneye and shoveler; occasional white pinkfeet or barnacle geese appear. White oystercatchers can be seen here occasionally and also in Morecambe Bay.

The North Channel seems to be the wrong shape to funnel into the Irish Sea and the Cumberland coast such large numbers of such birds as the autumn shearwaters, skuas and arctic gulls from the North Atlantic passage; they enter the North Sea and are seen off the north-east coast, with onshore winds.

The migration of summer fish from the south brought a 15lb 4oz bass to Foulney in 1956 and a 5½ft tope weighing 64lb in August 1959. A 35lb winter cod was taken at Whitehaven early in 1971.

Sea-water Life

In the Cumbrian sea the first sign of summer is the appearance of mackerel shoals off Duddon Bay in late May. A calm autumn with onshore winds brings the jellyfish from Selker Buoy into the Duddon estuary, and often in spring the sea gooseberries (*Pleurobrachia*) are common enough to foul the whitebait nets in the Ulverston and Kent channels, or strand themselves in a glistening ridge along the tide-line of Fleswick Bay. The increase of phosphates in the Cumbrian Sea since World War II, due to increased sewage disposal in the Irish Sea, adds to the food-chains and ultimately the fish; but in excess it causes algal blooms during the warm calm weather of summer and autumn after excessive rainfall. Blooms produced by proliferations of three toxin-producing dinoflagellates (microscopic single-celled plants with two whip-like threads) in the plankton are often mistaken for oil-slicks. The greenish-brown jelly-like slime of *Phaeocystis* or the 'soup' of white *Noctiluca scintillans* frequently cover large areas of sea; $1\frac{1}{4}$ million *Noctiluca* were counted in a litre of Morecambe Bay water. They cause the luminescence around one's seaboots. In September 1971 an extensive algal bloom from Anglesey to Millom in the Duddon estuary killed innumerable lugworms, an important fish-food around Humphrey Head, Flookburgh Channel and the Kent estuary. This shiny copper-brown bloom was provisionally identified as a species of *Gymnodinium*, which caused 'red tide' deaths in the North Sea and on the Atlantic shores, and can kill fish at a concentration of 3 million cells a litre.

The discovery of high levels of methyl mercury in American canned tuna was followed by a government survey of fish round the British coasts. The increasing pollution of the eastern Irish Sea by waste heavy metals dumped outside the 3 miles territorial limit, and industrial effluents from as far as Yorkshire and the Midlands, was shown by the fact that the second heaviest average concentration of methyl mercury (0·51mg per kg) was found in the fish between Formby and St Bees, and the highest

in Liverpool Bay. The Solway fish averaged only 0·24mg. No
connection has been found between pollution and the frequent
occurrence of harmless white tumours of virus-borne *Lympho-
cystis* disease marking older deep-water plaice, flounders and
occasionally codling visiting the Kent and the Leven estuaries at
St Bees and Solway. It has been noticed here since 1905.

Solway's rarer fish visitors have ranged from thresher shark
and porbeagle to horse mackerel, oceanic sunfish, bonito and
long-finned tuna, and from dragonet and sapphire gurnard to
common sea trout up to 31lb in the stake-nets. The flats at Silloth are the winter haunt of dabs, plaice, a few sole, solenette,
flounder and codling. There are whiting from October to
December and a few sparling in August as well as dragonets,
sand gobies, pogge, bib and common and Montagu's sea snails.
Shrimps occupy the Solway shallows to Maryport, sprats shoal
into the firth, but fewer herring now come in from the Irish
Channel in October to January, and fewer herring-trawlers use
Whitehaven. Bass and mackerel seldom reach as far in summer,
but many lesser-spotted dogfish and thornback ray are taken on
line. From Workington Bank to Whitehaven, fishermen find
plaice, winter cod (14 or 20lb), haddock, whiting, occasional mackerel, small rockling and summer codling. Off the north Cumbrian
coast there are lesser numbers of brill, turbot, angler, lemon sole,
sand ray, poor cod and monkfish, and rarer red gurnard. Eels
inhabit rocky places between Parton and Harrington and, due
to the freshwater Pow Beck, trout occur in Whitehaven's tidal
harbour. Most of the fishing takes place 10–15 miles west of
Whitehaven. Irish boats may be seen from St Bees fishing for
Nephrops or scampi, though fishing boats moored at night often
leave their fishing lights on. Lobsters and crabs are caught, but
I have not been able to verify the crawfish. Mussels and periwinkles appear among the rocks south of St Bees, and often a
few prawns. The fish are bigger here than at Silloth. A 35lb cod
was caught on rod and line at Whitehaven in January 1971.
Deformed hump-backed cod are sometimes caught.

There are over forty-two British records for sightings of

leathery turtles, and one found on Whitehaven beach in September 1960 is as likely to have drifted in with the jellyfish and Portuguese men-o'-war as to have been thrown off a ship. Most of the so-called porpoises reported offshore are the much commoner bottle-nosed dolphin, whose schools make their way north in spring and south in autumn. More occasionally the larger bottle-nosed whale, largest of local cetaceans, and the lesser rorqual visit the Cumbrian sea, and a stranded Risso's dolphin proves that this species also passes on its way to Shetland and back. Kendal Museum had a Greenland harp seal found in Morecambe Bay in January 1868. Another was stranded in 1874.

Shrimps in the Solway or Flookburgh area are preyed upon by lesser weevers and endure twice daily the ebb and flood of tide. They burrow by day until only the tips of their stalked eyes and their delicate antennae protrude, safe from predatory lesser weever fish, wader birds, the scorching sun or boisterous gale. At night they track down their food by scent, or move seawards as winter snow-water dilutes the sea around them. Spring snow-water from the mountains causes some dispersal. The number of little shrimps in spring predicts the autumn catch of larger females. The shrimping industry is cyclic, with periodic shortages, as in 1971.

We have bird and plant reserves, but none to conserve marine life. The north end of Walney Channel, rich in marine algae, is worth conserving. A biological survey round Scarth Hole, opposite Lowsy Point and Sandscale, found brown shrimps, prawns, crabs, gobies, rocklings, pipefish, plaice, sprats, sand eels, sticklebacks, grey mullet, *Macoma* and *Tellina* shells, polychaete worms (*Pygospio elegans*), and the immigrant Australasian barnacle *Elminius modestus*, which reached Britain on the bottoms of World War II convoys, as well as *Balanus balanoides*, tunicates (*Botryllus*), clams, mussels, cockles and limpets. Starfish are abundant predators on the mussel beds at Roosebeck in the Ulverston Channel. Lakeland's largest oyster, trawled from the Bass Pool on the west of Piel Island in 1971, measured 7in by 6in and was full of good flesh. The pink shrimp *Pandalus montagui* is occasionally present,

K

as are the common brown *Crangon*, variegated scallops (*Chlamys*), scarf and lemon weed, green shore crabs, spider crabs (*Hyas areneus* and *H. coaritatus*), and sea squirts (*Ascidiella aspersa* and *Cicna intestinalis*). Even off Barrow, depending on the state of pollution, polychaete worms (*D. bombyx*) and tubeworms (*Pomatoceros*) attach themselves to stones, and there are hydroids (*Hydrallmania* and *Diphiasia*), occasional sea squirts, sea urchins (*Psammechinus miliaris*), porcelain crabs, sea slugs, starfish, lemon weed and pipeweed. A haul from 7 fathoms revealed over 8,000 brittle stars (*O. fragilis*) and colonies of dead-men's-fingers.

Neolithic midden deposits of oystershells, winkle, mussel, cockle, limpet and pelican's foot at Drigg dunes, Haverigg and the north end of Walney, and of cockles and mussels in the pre-historic Badger Hole on Barrow Scout, near Warton, show the importance of the food of the seashore in early human settlement. The food-chains are extensive. The stomach of a cod caught near Piel Bar contained three prawns, a shrimp, a shore crab, two small eels, and a large piece of *Laminaria* seaweed. Another contained 32 complete shore crabs (the food of eiders). Flounders feed on the young cockles between Humphrey Head and Holme Island.

The scarce warm-water crab *Gonoplax rhomboides* was trawled off Walney in November 1968. It has been taken off Southport and the Isle of Man, but is commoner off the French coast. *Nephrops*, the Dublin prawn, or scampi, is found in the outer grounds.

Mackerel shoals, abundant outside Duddon Bar in June, disperse south to Walney in August and September. Plaice build up their numbers in Cumberland's inshore waters from February to late summer, and by October two-year-old fish leave for deeper water, only a few immature fish remaining to winter. One of a number marked off Whitehaven was recovered in the Dee estuary, but only 1·2 per cent went over 30 miles, the maximum being 35 miles. About 4·5 per cent went 20–30 miles, and over 60 per cent remained within 10 miles of their starting-point. Plaice tagged off North Wales, their ultimate destination, have been taken at Plumpton Viaduct and Humphrey Head. A marked Cumberland skate moved only 4 miles in $4\frac{1}{2}$ years.

Sole range from Duddon Buoy to north-west Walney and, like sparling, approach the southern estuaries in late summer and autumn. Near Barrow, boats sometimes take the scarcer pollack and pouting, and in 1960 a poor cod was caught at Holme Island. Inshore, gobies, lesser weevers, pipefish, grey mullet, butterfish, shanny and butterfly blenny are commonly caught in shrimp trawls.

Sprats are the most abundant clupeoid fish, forming the bulk of the whitebait on Cartmel Wharf and in the Kent and Leven channels, along with young Manx and Kilkeel herrings. Parasitic copepod crustaceans, the tiny *Lernæenicus spratlae* and *L. encrasicola* sometimes infest their eyes. Because of the relative shallowness of Morecambe Bay channels near Walney and Piel they have a somewhat different fauna. Thornback rays reach Ulverston and Arnside, small monks come in from the deeper Irish Sea. Flue nets 100yd long in Piel Channel have often caught up to 40 stone of flounders on a tide. Dabs are common below Ulverston battery and much of Morecambe Bay serves as a nursery for young flatfish. The alimentary canals of flounders in the Kent estuary showed they fed chiefly on cockle and *Macoma* molluscs and polychaete worms. Only 20 per cent of experimental nettings by sea-fishery biologists in the Kent estuary contained plaice, 79 per cent had flounders, and 44 per cent salmon or sea-trout smolts, particularly the latter. Freshwater eels were the fourth most numerous fish, and salmon fifth. Sparling and twaite shad are taken in flue nets at Kents Bank and the Leven estuary where the former spawn in autumn. The Kent channels vary, however, and the river some years flows out nearer Grange than in others.

Plaice spawn in the eastern Irish sea between Cumberland and the Isle of Man, and the inshore waters all around the Cumberland coast form a nursery for their young. Flounders favour the Kent and Leven estuaries, feeding like the plaice on *Macoma* and *Tellina* shellfish, shrimps, crab, ragworm, lugworm, etc. Water temperature and pollution greatly influence the distribution of marine creatures. The Ulverston Channel has a summer temperature of 12° C (54° F), and its shrimps decline as the water falls to 9° C (48° F) by the end of October, 6° C (43° F) by November, 4° C (39° F) in mid-December, and perhaps zero at the end of a cold December. Flounders are more adaptable. The strong tidal western side of Ulverston Channel scours Carter Pool, leaving a poor marine life—sparse *Fucus* and *Pelvetia canliculata* seaweeds, a few barnacles such as *Elminius modestus*, a postwar arrival, and the green grass-like threads of enteromorphous algae. Its sand has but a few *Macoma* and *Tellina* shells, more ragworms (*Nereis diversicolor*), and, among the rocks, periwinkles, the rock-slater *Ligia oceanica* and young green crabs (*Maenas*); but in the sand at the end of the slag bank are many tiny oligochaete worms and colonies of *Corophium volutator*. A mussel-bed lies off the Bardsea–Rampside coast road, and seed-mussels from 'South America' (Roosebeck) have been used to restock Menai in North Wales.

Chapel Island and the east shore have richer feeding for the flatfish, with more polychaetes, lugworms, *Nereis* and *Naphys*, small worms of *Glyceridae* or *Syllidae*, and *Macoma* and *Tellina* molluscs. From Conishead Priory to Cowp Scar the sandy mud is the haunt of sandworms, *Arenicola marina*, ragworms, *Macoma*, *Tellina* and the clam *Myas arenaria*. It is, therefore, popular with local fishermen for bait-digging. Small shellfish like the bivalves *Macoma tenuis* (especially on Cartmel Wharf) and *Tellina*, the gastropod *Hyrobia ulvae*, cockle spat, mussel spat (off Roosevelt scar) and the amphipod *Corophium volutator* form the main food of wader birds and the biomass off the estuaries, like Cartmel Wharf. The tube-building worm *Pygospio elegans* is also abundant there.

CHAPTER TEN

Conservation and Change

WILDLIFE IN THE Lake District faces many problems, as does the very landscape. Ruskin complained of the new railways unloading trippers like sacks of coal at Windermere, but now the M6 pours in an endless chain of cars, many of whose occupants have not come to see the birds and plants, but are looking for teas, toilets and commercial entertainment, and complaining if there is 'nobbut scenery'. Lakeland views are also being blocked by the building of houses in the woods, waterfowl are being driven off big lakes designated as public highways by speedboats, buzzards and peregrines are being disturbed by climbers and are leaving their rock-nests, and mountain plants are being pulled out to improve climbing conditions in more and more areas—there are 17 pitches on the great gully by Whin Rigg at the top of Wastwater.

As for the fauna, more and more badgers, glow-worms, red squirrels and roe deer are run over or injured in the night, and birds by day. It is unsafe to stand where, before World War II, I used to watch the woodcock roding at dusk along the road from Grasmere to Rydal. The hard hand of Man, which has worked against wildlife for 1,000 years, now seems prepared to extinguish some of it.

Wildlife will continue to change. Since we first heard the Mediterranean collared dove's voice beyond Coniston in 1959 (when it bred at Anthorn on Solway), it has colonised the three counties and is heard at Grange, Ulverston, Windermere, Egremont, Carlisle, Keswick, Silloth, Kendal and Barrow. It is attracted to Whitehaven's grain industry, and may become a pest. The colonisation of Lakeland came mainly from Merseyside, for birds marked in the colony by the Ship Canal at Ellesmere Port were traced to Silloth, Barrow and Appleby, and another from Old Trafford (Manchester) to Carlisle. A biological increase brought fulmar, merganser, goosander, bittern, black guillemot, kittiwake, chough, golden eagle and godwit to breed in our time. Introductions by fowlers added Canadian and greylag geese. The future is less secure for Bob White quail (an American partridge), introduced in recent years at Dallam Tower's Fairy Steps limestone-scar, than for Carolina grey squirrel and American mink intruding into the south from the Yorkshire dales and the Wyresdale hills of north Lancashire. Meanwhile, native blackbirds, great crested grebes and several titmice have increased as the ecological changes have favoured them.

The common gull's recent colonisation of south-west Scotland should extend into Lakeland, though it has nested on the border near Bewcastle, and the little ringed plover has bred in Westmorland as a newcomer. The green woodpecker spread to Yewdale, Cartmel, Bassenthwaite, and elsewhere following its increase in the Yorkshire dales; but corncrakes and nightjar have declined into becoming scarce birds. Birdlife faces many problems. On the debit side, climbers have taken peregrine eggs from Ennerdale and Kirkstone, legally-protected birds have been shot and I have seen chaffinches still tethered beside traps to decoy cage-birds. On the credit side, nest-boxes continue to extend the range of pied flycatcher and redstart in woodland, and the increased use of garden bird-feeding tables has maintained high winter populations of titmice and chaffinches.

Deer and badgers thrive under afforestation. Otters have declined for other reasons. As sea angling for sport has increased on the coast, slow-breeding skate and dogfish have declined through over-fishing. Motorways may replace the railways as distributors of wind-borne plant-seeds, and aliens will continue to arrive via rubbish tips or the harbours at Whitehaven and

Silloth. Creeping New Zealand willowherb and yellow American musk have colonised the hill streams in our time and *Spartina*'s stiff cordgrass has come to the muddy coast. But greedy collecting by trippers has reduced the wild daffodils from Silverdale to Backbarrow and even uprooted lilies-of-the-valley from Eaves Wood nature trail.

The purist may confine his attention to native fauna and flora, and the ecologist remove alien sycamores from his wood and check the wild spread of rhododendrons on the peaty hillside, but no field-naturalist can escape the growing confusion from aliens in the countryside. The modern habit of liberating surplus waterfowl from collections is an irritating confusion to ornithology, but in fact Man has been responsible for much of the present wildlife we see. The rare masterwort by a brook near Ullswater and in a hedge at Bordenside in south-west Westmorland is an alien intruder. Slender blue spring speedwell *Veronica filiformis* at Levens Bridge and elsewhere, and pink Claytonia, are garden escapes spreading widely in Lakeland, and should not command the respect accorded to the purple mountain saxifrage brightening Nab Scar and Loughrigg, though they may soon attract more attention, like the yellow Welsh poppy. The trade in Cumberland turf spread spotted medick and other plants. *Erinus alpinus*, a pink Swiss plant, has escaped from cultivation to grow outdoors, and Muncaster Castle's lost flamingos attracted more interest in Morecambe Bay and near Liverpool in recent years than the less conspicuous wild water pipit visiting Leighton Moss. The aim of the naturalist is to discover which plant and animal escapees are establishing themselves by breeding and threatening native species.

Butterflies which have either become extinct here or are at the precipice of extinction include ringlet, comma, wood white, large heath, brown hairstreak and silver-studded and little blues, while the marsh fritillary of May and June is confined to a very limited area of north-west Cumberland, near Solway.

Conservation raises questions about the effect of the extraction of limestone: local stone is being priced out of the building

market, except for decorative work like garden walls; but if we
prefer to see local slate roofs we must accept quarries in the
landscape. Now that people can spend more on their gardens
elsewhere in England, the demand for a limestone rockery in-
creases, however, and the increasing despoilation of south Lakeland hills by ruthless extraction of large lumps of water-worn
limestone for landscape-gardeners causes concern. The hills and
woods above Silverdale, Yealand Redmayne (Gaitbarrow
Wood), Warton, Grange-over-Sands (Hampsfield Fell), Arnside, Holme Park Fell, Newbiggin Crags and Farleton Knott
have suffered in recent years. Following a public inquiry in 1971,
the Minister of the Environment confirmed a Lake District
Planning Board enforcement notice on one estate against further
extraction on Hampsfield Fell, as 'it would not only harm the
visual amenities, but seriously affect the geological, ecological
and scientific value of the site'.

Then, what will happen if more water is taken from the lakes?
And can they take more water-sports, will new caravan camps
permanently reduce the local wildlife, and so on? Should action
be taken about the raised peat-mosslands which once sprawled
along Solway and fringed Morecambe Bay but have dried out
and been taken over by birch and bracken? The road has been
widened in the lovely Lyth Valley, but widening would destroy
the character of most—such as the one that winds up Dunnerdale
into Langdale.

Were it not for the sea-fisheries committees, little would have
been done about coastal pollution, except to pass resolutions.
Until recently the Lancashire committee also patrolled the
Cumberland coast. A worse threat than oil-slicks, which depend
much upon the direction of wind, as when the *Hamilton Trader*
slick drifted to the seabirds of St Bees, is the increasing deposit of
heavy metal salts and phosphates in industrial waste and sewage
in the eastern Irish Sea, including from 0·05–2·4mg of mercury
per kg, the second highest in British coastal waters. In 1971–2, a
sea-fisheries committee scientific survey of coliform (sewage)
bacteria in Lancashire coastal waters found 955cols per 10ml the

mean in counts in the Kent estuary at Grange-over-Sands, second only to Lytham on the Ribble (959), but far ahead of Heysham (10) or anywhere else.

The inshore waters, like the land, will change with the years and the marine life will vary with them. In north Morecambe Bay the great Yeoman's Bank has changed over the years, growing larger or smaller with the accretion and erosion of sand. This, as much as the severe winter frost in 1962–3, may have brought the decline of cockles to their present odd, scattered settlements, with the last big set at Cartmel in 1952 and the last of all at Silverdale. Estuarine barrages or storage reservoirs may alter the salinity of Morecambe Bay and Solway, and bring profound changes to the fish and birdlife, which would then inhabit static instead of tidal water. Shelduck might suffer most among duck of Morecambe Bay (along with greylag geese) as they feed mostly on small sea shellfish *Hydrobia*. Other wildfowl flocks are not so much tied to regular feeding grounds as are the massive flocks of dunlin, knot, oystercatcher and redshank. There would be some redistribution of duck haunts, excepting perhaps for an increase of teal and mallard. Cockles and shrimps would decline, but flounders could adapt themselves and there would be an increase in water 'fleas' and freshwater shrimps, trout, eels, perch, pike, minnows, and plants like reeds, sedges and Spartina. Wigeon would lose some haunts but gain from any polders planned—if recreation yachting did not upset all this. A sluice is planned for migrating salmon, but these fish are notoriously difficult to discipline to new routes. A barrage could hold the sea trout, which do not go far out to sea, and flounders, grey mullet and freshwater eels could tolerate the change; but the muddier modern shores at Grange and elsewhere would develop a different birdlife, because of different food and a rapid growth of marginal vegetation when currents cease.

These estuaries are necessary in the ecology of inshore life. Most of the catch of inshore fishermen spends an important part of its life in estuaries, spawning, feeding or developing. Tides will dilute estuarine pollution, but on the last leap of its long journey from the Greenland or Arctic Sea a salmon needs to find clear, clean cold water with sufficient oxygen in the upper spawning reaches. In law it has a right of way to this.

Conservation of wader-haunts in north Morecambe Bay is necessary, since these banks have been shown by ringing to serve as major resting places for autumn moulting by massed flocks of birds, especially knot and dunlin, which come here for this purpose after a brief stop on the east coast. On the Solway Firth conservation is required not only for the flocks of barnacle geese but for the Gerard's mud rush, creeping fescue, sea *Poa* grass and white clover that is their food.

Plastic pollution is a new problem. Even synthetic nets lost at sea continue fishing while drifting near the bottom, or entangled in rocks and wrecks: one washed up near Walney Island had caught nineteen dogfish, and another contained the drowned bodies of auks.

The use of fertilisers and the mechanisation of farming have come to stay. I have shown in lectures colour-slides of pastures near Carlisle made wholly green by the 'selective' extermination of all broad-leaved plants as well as their buttercups and daisies with MCPA, and of onion-fields there where the yellow flowers of charlock and all other broad-leaved plants have been entirely removed by the same weedkiller. But we must save the hedgerows for birds and control any *excessive* use of the more harmful —though often necessary—chemicals. Anyway, we cannot go back to the agriculture of our grandfathers.

The Eden and the Derwent salmon survived ulcerative dermal necrosis in the 1960s and 1970s, and rabbits the myxomatosis outbreak in the previous decade; but fauna and flora are seldom able to adapt to radical changes in their habitats. Also, as dead birds lay no more eggs, the birdshooter causes a permanent loss, unlike the quiet secretive birdwatcher. Knowledge is not a closed book, but it has been necessary here to withhold the precise locations of several rare plants and insects for their safety.

We may yet go back to the days of eagles and ospreys, however, despite increased tourism. Man is not a natural enemy of wildlife. It fears him because of his abuse of gun and dog. The coming of the roadside colony of bitterns at Yealland Storrs in full view of perambulating birdwatchers, the continued growth of Lancashire cranesbills among the trippers of Walney's Biggar Bank, and the increasing broods of mergansers dodging the boats on all the lakes illustrate how wildlife can meet the pressures of people—as long as people see no glory in killing live creatures, collecting eggs, or filching ferns and pressing wild flowers into herbaria. It is nearly fifty years since all three Lakes counties adopted a bylaw prohibiting the uprooting of ferns and flowers growing on land to which public has access, and the 1968 Theft Act makes it illegal to sell wild plants, rooted or not. The professional botanist has no prior claim on his specimens either, and too often he has been at the root of the trouble in his search for rarities. To many visitors unable to recognise the rarities, the robin on Ruskin's tomb at Coniston is just as welcome a sight as the rarest American wader at Grune Point, and Wordsworth's spring celandines are worth all the rare plants on the Red Screes.

Climatically and geologically Lakeland has seen its best days. The parade of the mammals has passed its peak, but the slow unending stream of evolution can still maintain the pattern of flora and fauna if we conserve sufficient habitats.

The evolution of the naturalist is of interest. He began as a tabulator and collector of species, interested chiefly in distribution, then assumed a wider interest in ecology and ethology, and finally turned into a professional, whose activity narrowed from the all-round competence of the old field-naturalist into that of the specialist knowing more and more about less and less. *Avis dictatorius* is the one species we wish was rarer.

Appendix One

DALEMAIN, Penrith: fallow deer—private (B5320)

DALLAM TOWER, Milnthorpe: fallow deer; heronry—private (B5282)

ELTERWATER: winter swans (B5343)

ESKMEALS DUNES PENINSULA, Ravenglass: Lake District Naturalists' Trust reserve

ESTHWAITE: North Fen reserve (grid ref 335.49718)

FELL FOOT: National Trust country park, 18 acres, south Windermere (A592)

FOULNEY ISLAND, Rampside tidal causeway, Barrow: 5 breeding terns, including roseate; plants, including *Mertensia*; wardened nesting season (SD 2463; A5087)

GLASSON MOSS: Nature Conservancy reserve, 140 acres; Solway; bog-moss; birds; insects

GLENRIDDING, Ullswater: pied flycatchers, etc (A592)

GRANGE-OVER-SANDS: *Meathop Marsh:* greylags; *Eggerslack, Witherslack: Lepidoptera; Whitbarrow, Scout Scar, Humphrey Head:* limestone flora, ferns

GRASMERE: winter diving duck, whoopers (A591)

GRIZEDALE deer forest, Satterthwaite–Hawkshead: deer museum; red deer and roe; polecat, capercaillie, blackcock, grass snake; camp site, etc; High Seat hide

GRUNE POINT and MORICAMBE BAY, Silloth: passerine migrations; nesting and passage waders, wigeon, greylags (NY 1456; B5307)

HALE MOSS: Lake District Naturalists' Trust reserve, 1 acre, N of Carnforth (near A6)

HAWES, Duddon estuary: greylags (A595)

HAWES WATER, Silverdale: calcareous shell-marl; *Primula farinosa, Pinguicula*, orchids, etc; bitterns

HAWKSHEAD, Esthwaite North Fen: grebes, etc (B5286)

HAYBRIDGE: nature reserve and deer museum, Low Haybridge, Bouth, Newby Bridge, 220 acres

HOLKER ('Hooker') HALL and Moss, Cartmel: fallow (menil) deer, red and roe deer; *Lepidoptera; Old Park Wood:* lime-rich clay (B5278)

HUMPHREY HEAD, Cartmel: aster goldilocks (northern limit), western spiked speedwell; waders (spotted redshank, etc) (B5277)

HUTTON ROOF, Burton-in-Kendal: limestone plants and moths (A65)

IVY CRAG WOOD, Under Skiddaw: Lake District Naturalists' Trust reserve

KENDAL: *Brigsteer Wood; Fisher Tarn*, birds; *Kentmere Valley and reservoir*, peregrines, winter duck, ravens, etc

LAKE DISTRICT NATIONAL PARK CENTRE: 32 acres, Brockhole (A591, Windermere)

LEIGHTON HALL—Storrs Moss—Silverdale Station—Yelland: RSPB reserve—reedbed bitterns, water rail, reed warblers, duck, visiting ospreys, marsh harriers, wild swans, waders; public hide (A6)

LEVEN ESTUARY: winter duck, goldeneye; *Flookburgh, Bardsea Wood Ulverston:* canal foot, etc (A5087)

LEVENS HALL PARK, Kendal: dark fallow deer; River Kent; sandpipers (A6)

LOWTHER CASTLE PARK, Hackthorpe, Penrith: 'wildlife park'; red, fallow, sika deer (A6)

LYTH VALLEY: damson blossom (May), flora; *Lepidoptera*; *Whitbarrow, Winster* (A5074)

MARDALE, via Hawes Water, Bampton and Shap: golden eagles, peregrines; deer

MEATHOP MARSH and WOODS, Kent estuary: Lake District Naturalists' Trust reserve; greylags in winter; *Cat Crag:* ferns (SD4481; B5277)

MERLEWOOD, Grange-over-Sands: Nature Conservancy woodland-ecology research station and northern headquarters (SD4079)

MOOR HOUSE: Nature Conservancy reserve and research centre, 10,000 acres, 7 miles S of Garrigill; east Great Dun and Little Dun fells, Eden Valley-Upper Tees moors, 1,825ft (Pennine Way, B6277)

MUNCASTER CASTLE, Ravenglass: azaleas, camellias, trees; exotic bird collection; deer, etc

NADDLE LOW FOREST, near Hawes Water: primitive ash, sessile oak and birch on slate in high rainfall area; 250 acres

NEWTON REGNY MOSS, Penrith (B5305)

ORTON MOSS (NW Cumberland) and SCAR (SE Cumberland), Tebay-Kirkby Stephen: Great Ashby Fell; grassy limestone. Bucknell Fell: Lake District Naturalists' Trust reserve (B6260)

PATTERDALE, Ullswater: for *Helvellyn*; *Angle Tarn:* red deer; *Glencoyne, Gowbarrow:* fell ponies (A592)

PLUMPTON QUARRY: Lake District Naturalists' Trust reserve; plants including ferns

RAVENGLASS (Drigg Point): local reserve via Drigg for Sandwich and other terns, black-headed gullery, etc (permits from Cumberland County Land Agent, Carlisle) (SD0497–0795)

ROANHEAD DUNES, Dudden estuary: flora (orchids, *Pyrola,* etc)

ROCKLIFFE-ON-SOLWAY: pinkfoot geese, etc. Lake District Naturalists' Trust reserve (NY 3464–3062)

ROUDSEA WOOD, Greenodd: Nature Conservancy reserve on limestone and slate; *Lepidoptera;* roe; fly orchid; *Carex flava;* 17 ferns including *Osmunda* and Ophioglossum; grass snakes, etc (SD3382; B5278)

RUSLAND MOSS, Furness: raised bog; roe; adders; spiders (*Maro lepidus*); nightjar; royal fern, etc (SD3388). *Moor:* mountain hare. 28 acres Nature Conservancy moss reserve

RYDAL WATER: winter pochard, swans, etc, greylags (A591)

ST BEES HEAD, via Sandwith: nesting auks, gulls, etc (May–June); gannets, shearwaters, etc; seabird passages; *Fleswick Bay:* sandstone-cliff flora (NX9413; B5345)

SANDSCALE HAWS, Duddon estuary, Dalton-in-Furness: orchids (coral-root, duneland helleborine), wintergreen, etc—dune flora; little tern

SCAFELL and PIKE: mountain flora; origin glaciers. Via Dungeon Ghyll, Mickleden, Rossett Ghyll, Angle Tarn, Esk Hause, etc (NY2209–2004)

SCOUT SCAR, Whitbarrow: limestone flora, badgers, etc (A5074 from Row)

SILVERDALE: *Quarry:* orchids (fly, dark-red helleborine) and limestone flora; *Elmslack—Waterslack—Middlebarrow Woods:* flora, red squirrels, woodcock (National Trust); *Black Dyke—Silverdale Moss:* flora (hellebore, etc)

SKIDDAW: *Ivy Crag Wood:* daphne, etc; small mammals; Lakes Naturalists' Trust reserve (A591)

STAVERLEY, Gill Wood: Dorothy Farrer's Spring, Lake District Naturalists' Trust reserve

STRIBERS MOSS, Haverthwaite: *Lepidoptera* (B5278)

SUNBIGGIN TARN, Ravenstonedale: winter duck (goosander), black-headed gullery (A685)

TARN HOWS: merganser, greylag, sandpipers, tree pipits, etc; *Wooded Hill Fell—Tarn Hows Gill:* woodcock, wood warblers, redstarts; glow worms; badgers

TILBERTHWAITE GILL, Langdale–Coniston (A593)

TOWER WOOD, Windermere: deer, badgers (A592)

WALNEY ISLAND (South): eiders, gulls, terns; flora (*Mertensia*). Lancashire and Lake District Naturalists' Trust reserve (permits needed); cottage accommodation. Road access by bridge, Vicarstown (A590)

WASTWATER SCREE: alpine plants (May–June); Wasdale and Kirk Fells (NY1810–2109)

WATERHEAD, Ambleside: Skelsghyll Wood

WETHERAL, Carlisle (Warwick Road): Eden Woods walk, National Trust, 21 acres, salmon, dippers, etc (B6263)

WHIN'S TARN, Penrith: winter duck (goosander) (A686)

WHINLATTER PASS: flora (B5292)

WHITBARROW SCAR, via Howe: limestone plants; 250 acres Lakes Naturalists' Trust reserve; 18 ferns Witherslack side; Flodder allotment site (A5074)

WINSTER VALLEY, via Lindale: butterflies (A590)

YEWBARROW, Furness–Finsthwaite, Newby Bridge, Bortree Tarn: yews, deer, etc

YEWDALE, Coniston–Skelwith, via Holme Ground, Hodge Close, Tilber-thwaite: tree pipits, dippers, pied flycatchers, green woodpeckers, redstarts, tree-creepers, buzzards, ravens (quarry), black-headed gullery (Low Oxen Fell Tarn), curlews; bogbean

SITES OF SPECIAL INTEREST

Geological sites: Ashgill Quarry, above Torver (Coniston); Bowder Stone (perched erratic block), Borrowdale; columnar basalt crag of Borrowdale Series, field 400yd SW of Rainor's Farm, near Gosforth (Grid Ref 308.503)

Gulleries: Bassenthwaite, Blaze Fell, Carlisle, Drigg Point, Faught, Greenside Tarn, Halefield, Heads Nook, Kirkby Thor, Leighton Moss, Low Oxen Fell (near A593, Skelwith), North Scales, Rockliffe, Skeggles' Water (Kentmere), Skinburness Marsh, South Walney Island (Barrow), Sunbiggin Tarn (Orton), Tarn House (Kirkby Stephen)

Heronries: Dallam Tower, Great Corby, Haverthwaite (Roudsea Moss), Muncaster Castle, Smardale Mill, Underfield Hall

Museums: Carlisle, Grizedale, Kendal, Keswick, Lower Haybridge (deer), Penrith

Nature trails: Brandholme (Lake District Naturalists' Trust, near Windybrow), Eaves Wood (Silverdale), Grizedale Forest (Ridding Wood), Laundry Ghyll (West) and Swirls (East), Skelghyll Wood (National Trust, behind Waterhead, Ambleside), Thirlmere Forest, White Common (National Trust between Rydal and Grasmere)

Wader flocks roosting (at high tide): Flookburgh, Foulney, Meathop, Moricambe Bay (Anthorn), Piel Island, Sandgate, South Walney

Appendix Two

ORGANISATIONS

Angling: Broughton (Workington), Carlisle (Eden), Keswick (Derwent and Greta), Kirkby Stephen, Milnthorpe (Bela), Ulverston, clubs and associations

Aquarists' Clubs: Carlisle, Whitehaven, Workington (West Cumberland)

Association of Lakes Counties Natural History Societies

Countryside Holidays Association (CHA): Grasmere (Forest Side), Ambleside, Borrowdale, Bassenthwaite, Eskdale (Wasdale Head), Kirkby Lonsdale (Lunefield)

Cumberland Geological Society

Cumberland River Authority, London Road, Carlisle. Includes Bassenthwaite, Derwentwater and Ullswater

Cumberland and Lancashire Water Authority—to replace present river authorities

Cumberland Sea-Fisheries Committee, Whitehaven

Cumberland & Westmorland Antiquarian & Archaeological Society (Kendal)

Deer Society (British), Lakeland Branch, Priory, Kents Bank, Grange-over-Sands, and Low Haybridge

Fell & Moorland Working Terrier Club, Egremont

Fell & Rock-Climbing Club of English Lake District

Freshwater Biological Association, Ferry House, Far Saury, Ambleside

Friends of the Lake District, Greenside, Kendal

Holiday Fellowship (HF): Monk Coniston, Portinscale (Derwent Bank), Skelwith Bridge (Newlands)

Lake District Naturalists' Trust, Park Road, Windermere

Lakes Defence Committee (Ullswater, Winster Valley, etc)

Lancashire River Authority, Northern Area, Halton. Includes Coniston Water and Windermere. Headquarters: West Cliff, Preston

Lancashire & Western Sea-Fisheries' Committee, at Lancaster University, Green Lane, Bailrigg, Lancaster

Lakes UDC, Ambleside

Ministry of Agriculture, Fisheries & Food: *Cumberland*—Eden Bridge House, Lowther Street, Carlisle; *Westmorland*—Eskdale House, Shap Road, Kendal

Mountaineering Clubs, Kendal, Keswick

National Park Information Centre, Church Street, Ambleside

National Trust information centres: Bridge House, Ambleside; Main Square, Hawkshead; Chapel Stile, Grasmere; Lakeside, Keswick (Cockermouth)

National Trust, Broadlands, Borrans Road, Waterhead, Ambleside. *Campsites*—Wasdale, Gt Langdale, Low Wray (Ambleside), High Wray, Park-a-Moor (East Coniston), Little Langdale Quarry, Wray Castle

Natural History Societies: Ambleside Field Club; Arnside NHS; Barrow Naturalists' FC; Carlisle NHS; Coniston NHS; Eden FC; Grange & District NHS; Kendal NHS; Solway Bird-Watchers' Society; West Cumberland (Whitehaven) FS

Nature Conservancy: Merlewood, Grange-over-Sands

Outdoor Pursuits & Field Centres: Brathay Hall Trust (Ambleside); Brantwood (Coniston); Derwent Hall, Portinscale, Keswick (Sunderland Education Authority); Howtown, Ullswater (Durham EA); Hawse End, Keswick (Cumberland EA); Lake Windermere (Manchester EA); Matterdale School (NE Cumberland); Outward Bound (Ullswater); Venturers' Forth Base, Cartmel; YMCA Camp (Ulverston)

Ramblers' Clubs: Carlisle, Whitehaven, Workington. Association area C (1 Piccard Street, Greaves, Lancaster). *HF Branches:* Barrow, West Cumberland, Carlisle, Kendal (with CHA)

Wildfowlers' Clubs: Egremont, Furness (Ulverston), Grange-over-Sands, Solway (Carlisle Branch), South Cumberland (Millom), West Cumberland (Workington), South Westmorland (Milnthorpe)

Youth Hostels Association (YHA). *Hostels*—Arnside; Black Sail and Gillerthwaite, Ennerdale Bridge, Cleator; Buttermere, Cockermouth; Carlisle; Double Mills, Cockermouth; Coniston (Far End and Coppermines); Crosthwaite, Kendal; Duddon, Seathwaite; Elterwater; Eskdale, Boot; Longthwaite and Grange-in-Borrowdale; Grasmere; Glenridding; Hawkshead; Loughrigg (High Close); Honister Hause; Kendal; Keswick; Kirkby Stephen; Nether Wasdale (Gosforth), Patterdale; Penrith; Rockliffe-on-Eden; Troutbeck

Bibliography

Agricultural Land Classification Maps. Sheets 75–88 Cumb; 89
   Lancaster & Kendal; 82–90 Westm Ministry of Agriculture,
   Fisheries & Food
Blake, A. *Solway Firth* (Hale 1955)
Brindle, A. 'Lake District Caddis Flies', *Changing Scene*, No 3
   (Penrith 1966)
British Fern Gazette, vol 9 (1965), 6
Clare, Davey and Macrae. *Introduction to Prehistoric Archaeology
   of North West England* (WEA, Liverpool, 1972)
Corlet, J. *Morecambe Bay Barrage Study, Biological Aspects* (Natnl
   Environmental Res Council, October 1970)
Cumbria (monthly, originally YHA, then Dalesman Pub Co),
   and its guides to northern and central Lakeland, Upper
   Eden, Ullswater, Grange, etc
Drinnan, R. E. 'Investigations into Feeding Habits of Oyster-
   catcher', *NW Bird Report* (Merseyside Naturalists' Assoc,
   1954–5), 30–2
Fell & Rock Climbing Club *Guides*: Dow Crag, Pillar, Gt
   Gable, Borrowdale, etc
Field Naturalist (Penrith, etc, NHS monthly, mimeographed
   1950–5, printed quarterly to 1968)
Frost and Brown. *The Trout* (1967)
Fullerton, J. H. *Solway Shrimps & Flounders* (Fisheries Bd, Scot-
   land 1889)
Geological Survey Memoirs: Maryport & District (1931)
Gibson, W. *Coal in Great Britain* (1927)

Glaister and Leitch. 'Flowering Plants of W Cumberland', *Trans Cumb Assoc* (1881–2)

Greswell, R. K. 'Glaciation of Coniston Basin', *Liverpool & Manchester Geol Jnl* (1962)

Griffin, A. H. *The Roof of England* (1968)
Pageant of Lakeland (Hale 1966)

Hardy, E. 'This Other Eden', *Salmon & Trout Assoc Mag*, no 154 (1958), 176–82
'New Salmon in Europe, Introduction of Pacific *Oncorhynchus*', *Salmon & Trout Assoc Mag*, no 163 (1961), 132–8
'Marine Fishes of Morecambe Bay', *Field Nat*, vol 13, (NS) no 1 (1968)
'Marine Fishes of Morecambe Bay', *Cumbria* (July 1969)
'Northwestern Bird Report', *Merseyside Naturalists' Assoc Jnl* (1950 et seq)
The Bird Lover's Week-End Book (Seeley Service, 1950)
Fauna & Flora of Lancashire, Official County Handbook (Burrows, 1950)

Harrison, F. 'Our Northern Mosses', *Trans Cumb Assoc* (1881–2)

Heln and Roberts. 'Relations Between Skiddaw & Borrowdale Volcanic Groups', *Nature* (Physical Sc Sup, vol 232, no 35, 1971)

Hervey and Barnes. *Natural History of the Lake District* (1970)

Hinchcliffe, I. *A Backwater in Lakeland (Mardale)* (Manchester 1928)

HMSO. *Lake District National Park; Stratiography of Northern England*

Hollingworth, S. E. *Geology of the Lake District* (1954)
'Glaciation of W Edenside & Solway', *Q Jnl Geol Soc*, no 346 (1931)

Hodgson, W. 'Flora of Ullswater', *Trans Cumb Assoc* (1881–2)
'Flora of Cumberland', *Trans Cumb Assoc* (1898)

Jackson, J. W. 'Finds at Dog Holes Cave, Warton Crag', *Lancs Naturalist* (1909–13)
'Shell Marl Deposits in N Lancs & Lakeland', *Lancs Naturalist* (1914)

Macan, T. *Guide to Freshwater Invertebrates* (Longmans, 1971)
   Biological Studies of the English Lakes (1970)
Macan and Worthington. *Life in Lakes & Rivers* (1969)
McGlasson, G. M. *Fishing Industry of Solway Firth* (Annan)
Macpherson, H. A. *Vertebrate Fauna of Lakeland* (1892)
Marr, J. E. *Geology of the Lake District* (1916)
Mitchell, G. H. 'Geological History of Lake District', *Proc Yorks Geol Soc* (1956)
Ratcliffe, D. A. 'Mountain Flora of Lakeland', *Proc Bot Soc Brit I*, vol 4 (1963)
Shackleton, E. H. *Lakeland Geology* (Dalesman Pub Co)
Shaw, W. T. *Mining in the Lake Counties* (Dalesman Pub Co)
Simpson, N. D. *Biographical Index of the British Flora* (Bournemouth 1960)
Smith, B. 'Glaciation of Black Combe District', *Q Jnl Geol Soc* (1913)
Thornthwaite Forest Guide (Forestry Com, 1952)
Trans Cumb & Westm Antiq & Arch Soc (1886 et seq)
Trans & Reports, Carlisle Nat Hist Soc (1912–60)
Wailes, G. H. 'The Plankton of Lake Windermere', *Ann Mag Nat Hist* (1939), series II, iii, 401–14
Wainwright, A. *Pictorial Guides to Lakeland Fells* (*Westmorland Gazette* publications, 1966)
Wilson, A. *Flora of Westmorland* (1938)
Wilson, J. O. *Birds of Westmorland & North Pennines* (1933)

Index